COLLEGE TO CAREER

Other Related Career Books by
Joyce Slayton Mitchell

Stopout! Working Ways to Learn
The Classroom Teacher's Workbook for
  Career Education
See Me More Clearly: Career and Life Planning
  for Teens with Physical Disabilities
Taking On the World: Empowering Strategies
  for Parents of Children With Disabilities
Be a Mother and More: Career and Life Planning
Computer-Age Jobs: The Computer Skills
  You Will Need to Get the Job You Want
My Mommy Makes Money
Making More Money: 55 Special Job-Hunting Strat-
  egies for Retirees

COLLEGE
TO
CAREER

The Guide to
Job Opportunities

JOYCE SLAYTON MITCHELL

COLLEGE ENTRANCE EXAMINATION BOARD
New York

For Ned and Elizabeth,
who are on their own road from college to career,
with love and hope

CONTENTS

SOURCES AND ACKNOWLEDGMENTS

The primary sources of information for *College to Career* are the 1986–87 *Occupational Outlook Handbook,* published by the United States Department of Labor, and young men and women on the job in every part of the country. In addition to the first-hand experiences gleaned from hundreds of personal and written interviews with women and men—most of them in the first five years of their careers—other career models are cited from *Forbes, Fortune, Ms., Working Woman,* the *New York Times,* the *Wall Street Journal,* and many trade and professional magazines and newsletters.

It is a pleasure to thank the many contributors to this book: young men and women who told what life is like in their careers. Enthusiastic thanks, too, to my many friends in the publishing department of the College Board, especially to the director of publishing, Sue Wetzel Gardner.

Joyce Slayton Mitchell
New York City
April 1986

PART
1

COLLEGE: A BEGINNING

CAREERS ARE DEVELOPMENTAL

How can you decide what you are going to be when you don't even know all the things there are to be? How can you decide what you are going to be when you aren't sure how much you like to do the things you've heard about? It's difficult to commit yourself to a career decision now when you aren't at all sure how your values and priorities will change over the years.

For many students, it is easier to think about what you don't want to be. Perhaps one thing you're sure of is that you don't want to be a dentist like your dad or an architect like your mom.

Your career decision will be easier if you realize that you *will* change jobs and directions many times in your life. You aren't choosing one career now to last you until your retirement. Just as your values and priorities have changed in the past five years, they will keep changing in the next five years and during the next 25 years. Look at the adults you know—your uncles and aunts, cousins, neighbors, and friends. Think about them. Ask them what their priorities have been at different stages in their lives. Ask about the moves they may have made from one part of the country to another, the changes in their jobs, in their families, in the money they made, the money they spent, and their changing interests during different periods of their lives.

Just as you yourself change in time, as a result of your experiences and the people you meet, the world of work is ever-changing, too. It used to be that a young man or woman could plan for one job or one career. But today the average young person can look forward to six or seven different jobs, six or seven minicareers, that will make up his or her lifetime of work. For example, you may start out as a salesperson, go into management in a real estate agency, leave all of that for a political

3

appointment in your state government, venture into commercial real estate in a resort area, expand into a job as a recreational developer—and even then you may be open for several more changes before your work life is completed. Many young people who were interviewed for this book are already in their second or third different job, and they are still in their twenties. Some are getting business training anywhere they can in order to have the experience they need to go into business for themselves. Others are making a change for higher-level jobs and more money. And still others are changing jobs to get a broader base of experience in business because they plan a management career in their future.

Something good happens to you when you realize that you aren't choosing the one and only right job, or wrong job, for you. You can use everything you experience to build what you eventually become. There is no way that you can, or even should, know now what your future will be.

With the attitude that everything counts, and that choosing your career is a long process, it may be easier for you to see how your schoolwork fits into this process. The subjects you are studying now, the sports you are playing, the music you are listening to, the summer jobs at which you are working, the friends you have, and the test scores you get are all part of your career development.

The decisions you make now—the choices you make concerning what to do this summer, next summer, what to do on weekends, what to do in your own family, what courses to take, what clubs to join, what extracurricular activities and recreation to participate in—*are* career decisions.

THE FOCUS IS YOU

One way to help decide what you are going to do is to get your focus off the outside pressures and back on yourself. You don't have to concentrate on possible prejudices and sex-role stereotypes, or on the school's expectation of you, or on career education, or on the world of work, the inflated economy, the national debt, or the changing labor market.

All of these things will be factors in your eventual decision, but what you most need to begin with is an exploration of your personal career opportunities, no matter what the external conditions and expected changes are.

WORKSTYLE OPTIONS

There are many ways to work. Flexibility in time is increasingly an option for you. You can work full time. Or you may wish to share a job and use the rest of your time to write, make furniture, or rear a child. You may want to work part time or volunteer some of your time. And you may want to create your own job. "Flexitime" is a concept that is becoming more widespread in industry. It means you can select the hours of the day you prefer to work; two-career families often arrange flexitime so that one or the other parent is always with the children at home. There is home-based work, growing as fast as people take their computers home. Compressed workweek is another option, often used in the summer to increase the hours in a four-day week in order to leave early on Friday.

Today young men and women have more options for lifestyle and workstyle alternatives than at any time in this country's history. You can choose either to work on your own and make all the money you need, or to agree that your partner will take the major responsibility for making money while you do something else, or anything in between. Focus first on *you* and the kind of life you want, and next on the jobs and time options to do them as you make your choices and work out your career.

ESPECIALLY FOR WOMEN

As wonderful as the eighties career opportunities for women are and as true as it is that women no longer have trouble becoming dentists, lawyers, business managers, or engineers, it's important to be aware that women are still making 64 cents for every dollar earned by men. It's important for you to know that as of spring 1984, 8.7 million women were raising an estimated 16 million children without fathers present in the home. It's important for college women to realize that one year after a divorce, a husband improves his standard of living an average of 42 percent, while the wife's income drops by 73 percent, according to a Stanford University study. Consider those facts carefully. They affect every woman. Most women over 30 know their need to make money. It's often young women who don't take the need for making money seriously enough— those who are still in school where they can do more about increasing their money-making potential than at any other time.

Almost no one talks about it—you probably don't either—but, if somewhere in your mind is the idea that someone else will be financially responsible for you, then you probably think you don't have to make quite as much money as your brother or your boyfriend. What is it that keeps some young women from aspiring to make money? You don't have to choose between sharing your life with someone and making money!

If and when you decide to marry, you *can* choose the kind of marriage that permits meaningful work for both husband and wife. You can choose an equal partnership marriage in which you may both decide what each of you will do. Cooking, making money, rearing children, painting the house, cutting the grass, doing the laundry are all necessary, all shareable, in order for the partnership to function. Equal partnership doesn't mean you both have to paint the house; it does mean that you will both decide who will do what on the basis of who is best at it, or who has the most time and interest in the job, or who hates it the least, instead of deciding on the basis of being male or female. Equal partnership doesn't mean you are both the same, or even that you could be the same. It means that you both have equal opportunity and equal responsibility to decide about rearing the children, about buying the food, about making money, and all the other choices that create a full life. A marriage where each person has some control over and participates in making family decisions is the only way a woman can be free to make educational and career choices.

What will your life be like five years from now? Ten years from now? Fifteen years from now? Will you be married? Will you have children? Will you be working? If you are like most women, you will be doing all of these things at some time in your life. Everyone, especially young women, should know that in the United States, almost half (48 percent) of all mothers with infants under two are employed full time outside their homes. The rate is even higher for mothers with school-age children under 18, where more than one in every two mothers (61 percent) is employed.

Women are working because, like men, they need money to support themselves and their children. Helping you aspire to and plan for a career that makes money is a goal of this book. How does a young woman go about choosing a career? After all, you probably don't yet know the answers to where you want to live, what the work opportunities will be, what your income will be, whether or not you will marry, what your husband will be doing, whether or not you want to have children, or how many you will want to have.

A career starts in early childhood and extends through retirement. There isn't any work you do that does not count as part of your career. Caring for babies and children, managing a home, fund raising, working as an engineer, or working part time in sales are all part of your career development. It's all work, even though some is paid and some unpaid, some part time, and some full time or overtime.

Work requires skills to be learned and managed. Many skills are transferable from one job to the next. Some transferable skills that you may learn at work are speaking, listening, letter writing, leadership, decision making, persuasion, and time management. Transferable career skills are learned everywhere, including in the family. Maintaining a home and raising children count toward your career development as definitely as work in the military counts, or work in apprenticeship, or in college, or the first years of a paid job.

With the attitude that everything counts—including motherhood—and that choosing your career is a long process, it may be easier for you to see how your school or family work or present job and interests fit into this process.

Many women are brought up differently and treated differently than men are, in both school and at work. Research shows that in order to succeed at work, women have to accept these differences—and the anxiety that goes with them—before they can seriously plan their career strategies. You may always be in conflict over achieving success in your career and being a successful mother. You may always be worried about personal criticism of your work in ways that don't bother your husband or male competition. You may always find it difficult to be assertive and initiate your business plan compared to the ease with which the men you know perform the same business behavior. In other words, women have to learn to manage by accepting the traditional conflicts of successful women. A woman must be able to say with confidence that she wants a career and that she is willing to confront the problems that she will have because she is a woman. This advice is not only for women planning to go into management, it is also for women intending to go into law, politics, theology, engineering, medicine, mathematics, science, health administration, educational administration, and *wherever the men are*. For wherever the men are is where the money and policy making are!

ESPECIALLY FOR MEN

Traditionally, a young man's focus in choosing a career has been very different from the focus of a young woman. The young man has been expected to support himself plus a family when he grows up. He has been encouraged to measure his success in terms of the amount of money he makes. Do you recognize your own expectations in this description? The more you understand how you are systematically set up for certain choices, the more you will see a chance to vary those choices.

It's easy to see how young men are groomed to fit the stereotype from the time they are children and are asked the question, "What are you going to be when you grow up?" Your earliest answer was probably, "a cowboy," "a fireman," or "an astronaut." Adults often keep pressing little boys about what they are going to be until they become grown-up wage earners. And in school, most elementary schoolbooks picture adult men continually at work. In fact, adult men are so hard at work that the impression school children get is that the only purpose in life for a man is to work, to take the total financial responsibility for his family.

Many teachers, counselors, and parents are not conscious of the fact that they are preparing boys to be "success objects" as they advise them to take a strong academic program with a lot of math and science, leading to a profession or business career in which they will earn a lot of money or prestige. But the unspoken assumption is that men must be primarily the achievers and providers rather than people who can choose to integrate their work life with their personal life.

Remember that you don't have to fit the stereotype. You can begin to see yourself developing as a whole person with many choices, rather than as a man who has to earn more than anyone else and constantly compete with his peers. In the eighties, you don't have to be a success object. You can endeavor to be successful at many things, not just making money; but of course you can choose that, too. You can be successful in your work and the other aspects of your life. You can be successful with your friends, with your family, in the community, in the arts and music, in sports, and in other hobbies. You don't have to define yourself only as the breadwinner or measure yourself by the amount of money you make. You can consider sharing the stress and responsibility of being a breadwinner.

You can look forward to an equal partnership with your wife. As equal partners, you may both decide what each of you will do. Cooking, making money, rearing children, painting the house, cutting the grass, doing the laundry are all necessary, all shareable in order for the partnership to function. Equal partnership doesn't mean you both have to paint the house; it does mean that you will both decide who will do what on the basis of who is best at it, or who has the most time and interest in the job, or who hates it the least, instead of deciding on the basis of being male or female. Equal partnership doesn't mean you are both the same, or even that you could be the same. It means that you both have equal opportunity and equal responsibility to decide about rearing the children, about buying the food, about making money and all the other choices that create a full life.

When you understand the options open to you, you won't be tied to the values of the man who says he is best because he makes the most money. When you value yourself as an individual, you can consider all the career possibilities on the basis of your interests, your abilities, and your hopes, dreams, and ambitions. You won't have to specialize too soon, as though the only purpose of life is to get to the top first. You'll be able to change careers as your interests change. You'll be able to redirect yourself as you grow. You'll be able to tie in your career with your family life. You'll be able to say, "Hey, wait a minute! I don't have to make the most money to feel that I'm successful. I can succeed much better in other ways." You can discover what kind of a guy you really are. You can work out your career with a partner, and enjoy having someone else help bring in the bread. You can be free to explore many job opportunities that are unique for you and the kind of life you want to live.

YOUR SKILLS ASSESSMENT

There are hundreds of jobs for you to investigate, and there are three basic career steps to organize your search. The first is to learn about yourself—to assess your own skills, values, and interests. The second is to learn about work, to locate your job opportunities. And the third step is to find the educational and job pathways that will lead you to where you want to go.

One of the purposes of education is to learn what you like to do and how well you can do it. You are discovering your skills in the classroom as you learn how adept you are at mathematics and languages, history and science. At the same time, you are finding out what you don't like and what you don't do well. In addition to learning content skills, such as how well you can handle physics and Spanish, you also learn your transferable skills—how well you read, study, speak, and write. These skills will carry over into all of your subjects, and also into many career situations.

You learn what your skills are by your own evaluation as well as by your grades and test scores. Although your school grades may indicate how well you will do in college, they won't necessarily measure all the skills you've learned. You can't possibly tell what you're going to accomplish in life merely by assessing your school grades and achievements. For example, if you rank fourth in your mathematics class right now, that doesn't mean that you'll be fourth in money-making ability in your age group 20 years from now. Grades in high school and college *do not* predict who gets to be the happiest, the most miserable, the richest, the poorest, or the most powerful, either in work or in family life.

To find out more about your skills, take a look at your everyday actions—not only what you say you like or don't like, but the things you actually *do* with your time. Think about the subjects you study in school, the tasks you perform at work, the things you do at home that really excite you, that make you feel special and make the time pass quickly. Notice what activities make you feel good, and what activities make you feel lousy and make you feel you can't wait to get *out* of there! Think about how your activities are related to having fun, to making money, to school or work or community achievement. Then, notice what skills are needed for the activities you love. Is time management one of them? Is decision making important? Is being your own boss and taking the initiative a part of your enjoyment? Do you get along with almost anyone, or with one group of people and not another? Do your activities involve getting others to go along with you? Do they involve staying with the project after you've already lost your initial enthusiasm?

Here are a few more pertinent questions:

- Do you prefer to work in a particular geographical situation or location?

- Do you prefer to work with particular types or ages of people?

- Is money your main goal? Is power?

- Do you think you would like a job that is short on money but long on prestige?

- Would you like a job where you can be left to work on your own? Would you like to be your own boss?

- Do you like structure on a job, with specific expectations and clearly defined responsibilities?

- What kind of physical surroundings do you prefer where you work?

- Do you mind traveling, or working nights and on weekends?

As you learn more about yourself, you will notice how you relate to others—your ability to get along with other students, your family, and your coworkers; your leadership abilities in class and on the job; and your ability to get along with authority, such as your boss, your teachers, your coach, and your parents. Of course your skills, interests, and values will change. In fact, work experiences in school often bring about major changes in how you feel and act. But even bearing these changes in mind, there is still a lot to be learned right now about your skills in school, at home, and at work.

HOW TO USE THIS BOOK

Part 3 of this book, Career Groups, describes job opportunities. Read about several careers in Part 3 that sound appealing to you. When one career in a group interests you, read about the related careers as well. Using the groups in this way may help you find new ideas. Also read "A Dozen Odd Jobs" in Part 2 describing jobs that aren't easy to categorize.

Sometimes young people in a business-oriented family tend to look only at business careers, or military and government if their relatives are active in those fields. Or perhaps someone in your family has said "you ought to be" a professor, or a dentist, or a new car dealer, and you may not like the idea. Explore career possibilities that *you* have in mind. After researching these possibilities, you'll either want to learn more, or be able safely to eliminate them.

DEFINING THE JOB

Each job description begins with a definition, followed by a report of the tasks involved, usually with examples from young people in their twenties or thirties who add their perceptions to the description. Each job lists the requisite educational, computer, and personal skills.

Computer Skills Ratings

The computer skills are rated from 1 to 6 indicating the skill level necessary for the job. A quick glance at the number will show the level required for any given job. The number will be followed by the particular computer task it represents. Here are definitions of these tasks:

Skill Level 1:

READ
Be able to respond to instructions printed on a monitor or terminal screen.

Skill Level 2:

READ   *ENTER*
Put new data and information into the terminal (also called basic keyboarding skills).

Skill Level 3:

READ   ENTER   *PRINT*
Reproduce information on paper, disk, or cassette.

Skill Level 4:

READ   ENTER   PRINT   *SELECT*
Choose and know how to use word processing and integrated packages of software programs for different job needs. For example, an accountant may use a word processing program for writing reports and a bookkeeping program for keeping accounts.

Skill Level 5:

READ   ENTER   PRINT   SELECT   *GRAPHICS*
Use computer-aided design (CAD) or computer-aided manufacture (CAM) graphics programs to draw up engineering, architectural, electronic, or other plans and projections or to create illustrative material. Minimal knowledge of one programming language.

Skill Level 6

READ   ENTER   PRINT   SELECT   GRAPHICS
PROGRAM PROFICIENCY
Writing your own programs is a top-level skill in computer science. There are many levels of programs that can be written, but knowledge of three or more languages and ability to construct the functions that you want to use are the minimum requirements of a programmer. Skill level 6 requires knowing how computers work, being able to use several different computers, knowing how to program, how to analyze systems, and how to be comfortable with a great variety of computer functions.

How Many People Work in the Field

Information about the numbers of people in each career is next in the description, citing women and blacks whenever that information is available. This entry also gives specific numbers or percentages of people working for the various types of firms or agencies and the primary geographic locations of each job.

The Money Factor

As you research careers in *College to Career,* notice that the average salaries are cited for each career. It is easy to think of the average as the exact salary at which you can expect to start working. For example, in 1985 electrical engineers with a bachelor's degree started at an average of $26,556. What that average figure really means is that some engineers started at $21,278 a year while others started at $31,278. Beginning engineers *averaged* $26,556. For a better idea of the money you can expect in a particular career, you will want to translate the average salary into a range of starting salaries. Within this range, the particular salary you start with will depend on the college you attended, your college record, your work experience, where the job is located, and the type of employer.

If you are a student now, salaries will be even higher by the time you are ready for the job market because of inflation and cost-of-living salary increases. To give you an idea of the future rate of increase, let's look at past salaries for teachers. In 1981, they averaged $17,725, and in 1985, they averaged $24,276. Remember, when you read "average," that means many people make less and just as many may make more than the figure cited.

As you choose a career, what does money mean to you? Will your income be high enough to maintain the standard of living you want and justify your education costs? How much will your earnings increase as you gain experience? Like most people, you probably think of earnings as money. But money is only one type of financial reward for work. Paid vacations, holidays, and sick leave; life, health, and accident insurance; and retirement and pension plans are also part of the total earnings package. Some employers also offer stock options and profit-sharing plans, savings plans, and bonuses.

Which jobs pay the most? This is a difficult question to answer because detailed information is available only for one type of earnings—wages. Obviously, some kinds of work pay better than others. But, many times, the same kind of work does not always pay the same amount of money. Some areas of the country offer better pay than others for the same type of work. For example, the average weekly earnings of a beginning computer programmer vary from city to city. Generally, earnings are higher in the north central and northeast regions of the country than in the west and south. You should also remember that cities that offer the highest earnings are often those in which it is most expensive to live.

Earnings for the same type of work also vary according to the type of organization you work for. For instance, Ph.D. chemists in marketing and production earn more than Ph.D. chemists in industrial research and development; however, those in industrial research earn more than chemistry professors, who also do research.

You will undoubtedly wonder what the economy will be like when you enter the labor market. Each career description anticipates your chances for getting a job through the 1980s. These chances are estimates developed by the United States Department of Labor, and they are based on observable trends and general assumptions about the future of the economy and country. For example, some of the assumptions are that there won't be a major war or energy shortages, federal money paid to state and local governments will continue to decline, and current technological and scientific trends will continue.

Finally, you should remember that job prospects in your community or state may not correspond to the description of job opportunities given here. The opportunities in your area may be better or worse for the particular job you are interested in. The local office of your state employment service is the best place to ask about employment projections in your area.

Related Careers

This category gives you suggestions for other careers using similar skills and interests. Go ahead and read the related descriptions to broaden your choices.

More Information

Write to the professional group cited and you can expect to get a list of approved schools or colleges for that career. Most have career booklets and information written especially for college students and many will suggest books about their particular profession.

After you have looked at all the possibilities, choose one or two or three careers that sound interesting enough to read about and research further. Reading in detail about a career is a reliable way to acquire accurate information.

When you have read the career descriptions that interest you, look in your school and public library for trade magazines related to the career you are researching. If you want the inside story of what people in a career are reading, thinking about, and actually doing, read their trade magazine! The *Wall Street Journal, Variety,* and *Veterinary Economics* are where you will find out what people in the financial, theater, and veterinary worlds are really involved in. It isn't academic theory but the business of the job itself that you'll find in the trade magazines. In addition to learning what people in a career are doing, you can't beat the trade magazine as raw material for a job interview. For example, nothing will impress a book publisher more than hearing you discuss facts about his or her business that you acquired from reading *Publishers Weekly;* or a physician, if you can talk about the latest research published in the *New England Journal of Medicine;* or a banker, if you have the latest economic reports from the *American Banker;* or an urban planner, if you are aware of recent urban trends in *City.*

If your school library doesn't have the trade magazines that interest you, check your community public library or a local college library. Ask the reference librarian to help you select the trade magazines that relate to the job you are researching.

CAREER INTERVIEWS

It makes sense to talk to others who are willing to discuss their work to find out about a career. One good place to find people to interview about their work is in your own family. Ask your parents, aunts, uncles, and their friends to help you find people who are already in the career you are thinking about entering. Go and talk with them. If a securities salesperson is what you want to be, talk with a stockbroker and ask what it's like to be in securities. Does it sound like your kind of job? Ask another salesperson what it's like. How much of the job is fun? What parts of the job are awful? Listen to everything you hear, because *you* are the one who will be selling and either enjoying the hustle and competition or getting an ulcer by the time you finally make the sale.

In addition to your family, many of your teachers and professors will be good sources for finding people in careers that you are ready to research. Your clergy, youth group leaders, and others in your community, including the alumni from your school, will often want to be helpful to you. Go ahead and ask your network if they know a forester, a computer systems analyst, or a foreign service officer you can meet and interview in your career research. Don't wait until you are choosing a graduate school or hunting for a job to talk with others about their work. The more experience you have talking with people in careers that interest you, the more background you'll have for your decisions ahead. Not only will your interview experiences be good information right now, they will also be great practice for the crucial job interviews you will be having later.

Even though you don't know someone you have read about in the paper, go ahead and write to that person, saying that you are interested in learning about his or her job or in working during the summer or school holiday. Usually, people are flattered by your interest. In this way, you can learn how to make your own opportunities for future interviews and jobs. As a student, you are in a good position for exploring. You have a positive image, and people aren't threatened by you—they don't fear that you will take over their job. So, make the most of your learning status to learn about careers from the people already doing well in them.

When you have names of people to interview, call them. Tell them you would like to talk with them for a specific amount of time, so they will know you won't keep them too long from their work. Say, for instance, that you are interested in being a computer programmer and would like to talk about what the job is like with someone who knows. Ellen J. Wallach, author of *The Job Search Companion,* suggests that you make an appointment, then have the following questions in mind to help begin the interview:

- How did you get into this career?

- How did you view the work before you got into it? Is your view different now? How is it different?

- What do you like *most* about your work?

- What do you like *least* about your work?

- Why did you choose this type of work?

- What are the greatest pressures, strains, and anxieties about your work?

- What special problems might someone new to the job have in adjusting to it?

- Would you make the same career choice again? Why?

- Besides the environment in which you work, where else could someone perform your work?

- Are there other careers related to your work?

- How much time do you spend with your family? Is this amount what you expected to spend when you began working in your career?

- How much time do you spend with hobbies?

- How do your family and friends fit into the lifestyle your career creates?

- What are the greatest "highs" about your work—what really turns you on about it?

End the interview, advises Wallach, with, "Is there anyone else you know who also does your kind of work who might be willing to speak to me? May I use your name when I call?" And when you get home, write a short thank you note to the worker for sharing his or her time and work with you. This follow-up is a must.

Through your career-research process, remember that everything you learn counts. Even if you decide that a given career isn't what you had thought it was, you are still ahead by having accurate information. You may learn about new careers indirectly, and your follow-up from reading and interviews may lead you in directions you didn't plan on taking. The more information you finally have for your career decision, the more sure you can be of making the right decision—at least for this phase in your life.

STUDENT JOBS

Choosing a college major, and choosing work experience, are educational pathways or directions toward your career development. Your actual work experiences provide opportunities where you can try out your school concepts in a work situation.

Once you get a career idea that makes sense for you, use your summer vacation, afterschool time, and weekends for a trial run in that career, whether it's paid work or volunteer work. Work at a car agency if you are interested in sales, or in a hospital if you are interested in health care. Work with a children's group in a day camp or child-care center if you are interested in education, or in a bookstore or publishing house if the book business interests you. Try a summer job in a bank or real estate office if finance is your interest.

Even though the kind of work you are likely to get is the lowest level in that field and, therefore, reserved for beginners, the menial tasks become meaningful if you apply what you learn to your own career development. Even if you are doing a repetitious job that takes little thought, you can look around at the whole organization and notice the next step up for people who have permanent jobs and can get promotions. Who is your boss? Who is the top boss? Do any of those jobs look interesting? For example, a summer job in a real estate office may consist of painting front doors on homes to be sold. But you can look around and see the hours kept by the salespeople, listen to the kinds of questions clients ask and the answers salespeople give, and notice which salespeople are making the most money, which are putting in the most time, and which are living a life you would like to live.

Getting ahead in a job is like learning to walk or to ski. You've got to put so many hours and so many miles into learning, no matter who you are, or how fit you are, or how well qualified you are. When you start summer work, or an afterschool job, or your first full-time job, you will probably start at the bottom. Setting goals is what people do who really want to get ahead. It's especially important when you just begin a job and it turns out that the job isn't everything you had hoped it would be.

Your work may not always seem related to where you want to end up. But when you see how everything about a job counts, then your present work activity takes on new meaning. When the apprentice architect understands how he or she can use training to get ahead, then the tedious job of drafting other people's ideas becomes more meaningful. Your purpose in career exploration and development is to help you determine all the possible directions for your future.

STOPOUTS

Another work alternative, other than summer and afterschool jobs, is an internship or voluntary program for an academic year. An internship is a supervised work experience where the student can learn about a career or field of interest. Usually the student is not paid, but often he or she can earn college credit. Some students "stop out" of school for a year after high school or after their first year of college to test a career idea. A Princeton junior stopped out and took a job as a hospital orderly for ten months; she returned to school convinced that medicine was her vocation and that she wanted to be a doctor. Even though a medical orderly's job is very different from a doctor's, she learned about medicine as a *system*, about the different jobs within it, and became certain about the job she was after.

Doug Patt, from the University of California at Santa Cruz, stopped out of college twice to see what the world of work was like. His second stopout included a job in a management agency for recording artists, where he learned about the music business on his own. He also toured with a blues singer. When he returned to college, he had a practical sense about the career he had chosen: film production. What does he say he learned? "I learned that if you want something in business, you've got to go for it." A basic guide to information about internships during the academic year is *Stopout! Working Ways to Learn,* by J. S. Mitchell. Another is *1986 Internships: 34,000 On-the-Job Training Opportunities for All Types of Careers,* edited by Lisa S. Hulse. Both are available from Garrett Park Press, Garrett Park, Maryland 20896. A stopout placement agency for member colleges and universities is Venture, located at Brown University in Providence, Rhode Island. Specializing in undergraduate internships, they provide jobs for hundreds of students in business and in nonprofit organizations.

Internships, apprenticeships, and voluntary jobs while you stop out from college are like college credentials and paid jobs. They are all valid educational pathways in your career development.

CHANGING CAREERS

Some of you are already out of college and are now looking for that second or third job. You have already had some work experience. You want to consider a new career group, or learn more about a related job in your own group.

It used to be that an accounting major would go into accounting and stay there. A man would become a successful salesperson, perhaps switch companies, but never dream of leaving sales. A young woman would choose to become a teacher and then would teach until retirement. Nowadays, the accountant may change to a computer career, the salesperson may open his own business, and the teacher may change to an entrepreneurial career in real estate development. Today, a new group of job seekers has entered the job market. This new group is not made up only of graduate students, or the 8 million unemployed, or the 2 million homemakers who are looking for jobs each year. For the first time many job hunters in the United States are fully employed adults in career transition. Career changes in midlife are a new American phenomenon. The National Institute of Education reports that each year 40 million adults, or 36 percent of our working population, are in career transition. Most of those who change careers are between 30 and 59 years old, with the average being 38 years old. They cite financial need as the primary motivation for changing careers. Other reasons are: overcrowded career fields, early retirement, women entering the work force from home, attained career goals, failure to be promoted, and no possibility for growth on the present job.

If you are in the market for a new job, the principles of going after what you want are the same whether you are a student, a full-time parent, or a full-time employed worker. You need to know what you have—to assess yourself; what your career options are—to research the job market; and how you can get what you want—to acquire job hunting strategies that include how to locate the person who can hire you, how to write a résumé, to interview successfully, and to negotiate salary and promotion. Your personal assessment should include:

- Your transferable skills (problem solving, budgeting, analyzing)

- Your content skills (engineering, home management, computer programming, advertising, business)

- Your interest areas (paid and unpaid activities, hobbies, sports, clubs, leisure-time activities)

- Your lifestyle values (friendships, family, children)

- Your ideal job in terms of skills, interests, values, and purpose in life

- How your skills, interests, and values relate to specific jobs

To begin your research of the job market, read the job descriptions in this book. If one job interests you, look at similar jobs in the same career group. Next, follow through your search by writing to the professional associations cited for each career. Go to the library and look for a related trade journal. Translate what you learn about a career to your local level, or to the geographic part of the country in which you want to live. Finally, remember that changes in life tend to "rock the boat," even good changes. Handling change is easier with the support of friends and family. Reaching out to the people who care about you as you plan a career change will help smooth the transition.

Career change is one more way to look at your career development. As soon as you make a career choice, chances are that a change is going to follow. Plan for those changes. Think about what you are learning now that will keep your change options open later. Career change is a fact of career development. You can count on it.

KEEPING YOUR OPTIONS OPEN

Four-year college students and graduate school students can put off specific or specialized career decisions longer than two-year community college or technology students can. If you are a four-year student, or if you are stopping out from school, take advantage of this extra time and explore your options as best you can. Keep in mind that all the technological and economic changes you've heard about in the job market in the past five years are still going on. All the changes in you that you've noticed are still going on, too. In other words, in the next few years, it can be a whole new ball game. If you stick with assessing your own skills, getting in tune with your values and interests as they change in your personal life or work life, and if you keep your career options open for new directions, you can't go wrong.

PART
2

SOME
SPECIAL FACTS

CAREERS BY THE DOZEN

A DOZEN OF THE FASTEST GROWING CAREERS

The U.S. Department of Labor announced at the end of 1985 that the fastest growing jobs in the eighties for the college educated are these:

1. Computer programmer
2. Computer systems analyst
3. Electrical and electronic engineer
4. Travel agent
5. Physical therapist
6. Securities and financial services salesperson
7. Mechanical engineering technician
8. Lawyer
9. Corrections officer
10. Accountant and auditor
11. Mechanical engineer
12. Registered nurse

A DOZEN OF THE HIGHEST PAYING CAREERS

A number of facts were taken into account to get these figures. The averages may vary but you can be sure that if you want to go for the big bucks, you can find them here:

1. Major league baseball player: $289,194
2. Investment banker: $200,000

   3. Chief Justice, U.S. Supreme Court: $104,700
   4. CEO (chief executive officer): $98,500
   5. Physician: $97,700
   6. Airline captain: $95,000
   7. Dentist: $75,550 median
   8. Financial planner: 60 percent earn over $76,000
   9. Lawyer, corporate: $85,000
   10. College president $70,000 + $37,000 benefits
   11. Auctioneer, New York City star: $100,000
   12. Stockbroker, superstar: $300,000 to $1,000,000

A DOZEN OF THE HOTTEST BURNOUT CAREERS

The hottest burnout careers demand that employees control the uncontrollable, that they are always right. Burnout careers are often shortened because of heavy emotional demands. Something has to give—either the job or the attitude leading to burnout. They are listed in order, starting with the most demanding:

   1. Air traffic controller
   2. Nurse
   3. Doctor
   4. Junior high school teacher
   5. Elementary teacher
   6. Psychologist
   7. Retail buyer
   8. Stockbroker
   9. Social worker
   10. Truck driver
   11. Insurance manager
   12. Lawyer

A DOZEN ODD JOBS

Stretching Your Imagination

Your aunt introduced you to her new husband, a passenger acceptance coordinator. You remember her first husband well; he was a financial analyst. Your neighbor told you that his daughter just got a job as a publicist for a New York publishing house; her older sister is a hydrologist. Your best friend told you that his brother got a promotion to senior art editor. Maybe you know what all of these jobs are, but if you don't, you're not alone.

When a law student becomes a lawyer, a medical student becomes a doctor, an education major becomes a teacher, and an anthropology major becomes an anthropologist, it's easy to understand. They are following a clear line that we recognize. It makes sense. But what happens to all of those English majors? And history and psychology and math majors? And what happens to art history people?

Just think. Over half of all college graduates don't go into a career that is even related to their major. Do you ever wonder what they do? What becomes of them? How they know what to look for? What interviews to go after? And what about the 20 percent of last year's class who are unemployed? How do they know what jobs to look for now that they are out of college, and not near the campus recruiters and placement office?

The careers in *College to Career* are arranged by groups— Arts, Business, Health, Education, Social Service and so on. You will find the career you want to read about by the group you expect it to be in. You expect to find doctor, nurse, physical therapist under health careers. You expect to find real estate sales, stockbroker, new car salesperson under sales. But where would you expect to find publicist? What does a management consultant do? How does an adventure tour operator get into that kind of work? Because jobs don't usually follow a college curriculum, a dozen odd jobs were added to stretch your imagination from logical career groups to jobs that accept a great variety of college majors; jobs that people often "end up in" rather than plan to go in to; jobs that are the outgrowth and offshoot of working circumstances that sometimes give a person a new career idea based on work experience rather than on academic work.

Read about these special situations for what they say. Read them, too, for a small sample of the broad range of jobs that are out there for you to consider. When you meet that new uncle, your neighbor's daughter, or your best friend's brother and they come up with an odd job, ask about it. Find out what it's like to be a senatorial aide, what the day in and day out tasks entail, what the responsibilities, the hours and weekends and nights are like. Look into odd jobs. They can lead you to others that may be just right for you. Just because you can't define it doesn't mean you won't like it. Who knows? You may be proud to end up in an odd job!

Senatorial Aide

"I became a paid staff member right after Senator Patrick Leahy of Vermont was elected. The way to become a senatorial aide is to work on a *winning* election campaign. Even though everyone else on the campaign handed in a résumé (and it seemed as if everyone wanted the same job), I had been an outstanding worker and agreed to take anything. I was hired as a legislative and economic development assistant. The two skills that helped me most in my job were writing, which was one of the reasons I was hired, and a summer internship I had had with Common Cause, giving me a taste of how legislation works in Washington.

"It's a hectic pace, often 10 hours a day, extending into the weekends, especially at campaign time. I worked on human rights legislation that I found very fulfilling and rewarding. There were a lot of other idealists working in Washington. Even though the money doesn't begin to match the private sector, there's great pride and a feeling of accomplishment that society as a whole benefited from the legislation being passed because of our work. I'm leaving politics for business school, but I know that a lot of this job will never leave me. I view my career as an education; if I'm not learning something new, it's time to change jobs. I learned a lot about the political system in six years, and I learned a lot about myself at the same time. My biggest adjustment from college to the working world was realizing that the work I was doing had a public image. What I wrote and how I conducted myself reflected upon a United States Senator—that made me a lot more careful and responsible. In a lot of ways becoming a senatorial aide is like being in the arts—it takes a lot of luck to get the first break."

Set Designer

"I work for a design company in New York that does TV commercials. I got the job when I was taking a course at Parsons School of Design. One of my professors worked full time for a design company and taught one class at night. She thought I was doing such a good job that she hired me to work part time at her company. Starting part time for a particular project, I worked on the sets of five different commercials before I was hired full time.

"Hustling is very important in the design business. Studio time (renting a broadcasting studio) costs the production company thousands of dollars a day. When we go in there to design a set for the next day's shooting, we often stay until two or three in the morning. We can't do our thinking and planning in the studio; it has to be done before we get there—there is no tolerance for mistakes and things not going right on studio time. I wasn't really prepared for this job in college—college was so low-keyed and so easy on me—nothing like the minutes ticking off at high dollars for everything we do here.

"Now I need to learn some business skills to go along with my set designing. I'm not too good when talking to clients, but I'm listening a lot and trying to learn how to make the clients happy, so they will come back again to the same design company."

Software Engineer

"I didn't do well at all on my first job. It was nothing like college and I just wasn't prepared. In college it was just me and the computer working things out. I depended upon myself to get my work done; I was competing with everyone else in the class. On my job, we work cooperatively in groups of three or four for each software programming project. We are a team and have to give reports to each other. We have to depend on each other to get our work done and we have to be excellent communicators. I didn't have any experience in working problems out together, or in teamwork, sharing the results and phases of the program. I'm not good at communicating with others; I don't have any confidence at all when it's my turn to present my work to the group.

"I was told in college that computer programming was one of the fastest growing careers there is. That's true, but it doesn't take many people to develop the program! The software companies are not hiring a lot of new people. Small, well-communicating groups get all the work done. Since losing my first job, I have started graduate school, I have taken a public speaking class, I am playing team sports, and I got a job for a clock company that designs 'embedded computer programs.' That's where the jobs are. These embedded programs make up the major portion of all programming jobs around the world. Programs are "embedded" in a burglar alarm or a power plant system. Also washing machines, television sets, and lighting systems run by microprocessors all have software built in.

"I learned more about work in the first month out of college than I learned in four years. I'm working hard at becoming a team player. I find much more satisfaction in it, and look forward to group process, now that I know what it's all about."

Adventure Tour Operator

"This job is something like being a travel agent, only better. A group of us planned a whitewater rafting trip followed by a Colorado winter mountain climb our senior year in college. We were hooked; we decided that adventure tours beat going to business school for an MBA. We had come from liberal arts, not a business course among us. But we were strong in our determination to solve problems, work together in sports, and put in the necessary hours that it takes to start a new business.

"As exciting as it is to plan and lead adventure tours down rivers in canoes, on ski trips, and survival vacations, the task I had to take on was how to get enough clients on our tours to keep three of us in business, one part time. My job was outreach, bringing in the clients. I worked on getting corporations, professional groups, and university recreation departments as well as individuals. We got enough to get started, but broadening our base for bringing in the business still takes most of my time. I write proposals for new groups. The bigger the corporation, the longer it takes for their decision. Marketing our tours has to be creative because we are competing with travel agents and people planning their own adventure tours.

"A complete service is what we offer, beginning with solid information about the adventure; bus or plane transportation to the site; instruction for the adventure: skiing, rafting, hang gliding, sailing; and an opportunity to be as adventuresome as one chooses. We also plan so that a participant can soak up the sun and watch others; they don't have to participate to buy the tour. This is especially important when professional groups or corporations buy our tour. If there's too much pressure, the adventure feels like work! On the other hand, we believe in our adventure, and naturally reassure our clients that sports, adventure, and travel will make their vacation. We've been in business for four years and none of us has had more than one week off, but we're just about to change that.

"We're going to look around, take some time, and analyze our progress. We've concentrated on domestic tours, and now we are going to make a move to take on Third World tours or we are going to buy some buses, lodges, woods, and own some of the places where we take our clients. In many ways, it's a business like others; in other ways it's doing what we all love, adventure and travel. I'm here to stay, even though we'll probably often change directions and goals."

Concert Promoter

"All you need to be a concert promoter is a telephone, a state entertainment license, and a gift of gab. I started out with a concert promotion agency in San Francisco where I learned the ropes. I dropped out of college after my third year when I noticed I was spending more time following the rock concerts than going to class. I had worked on the entertainment series in college and the contacts I made helped me to get started. The first job you get is to book local bands. They say, 'Here's the talent, get out there and book them.' You have to be creative to sell tickets. You have to come up with something new all the time to get the media attention.

"Ticket sales are the best way to make money. Other ways include concession stands, but you don't always get the concession. The concert promoter has to hire and pay for everything, from rent to security, from ticket takers to stagehands. I set up a team of people that handle certain specifics: the security, the electronic sound, a production manager to handle stagehands and crew.

"I put in about 10 hours a day, six days a week, and more if I am doing two or three shows at once. I spend most of my time on the phone. I work with everybody—I meet the bands and their managers and agents. I meet radio people, police chiefs, and lawyers. The two things I really like about my job are the people I meet and the money I make. Being in the entertainment business is fun; it's always interesting and exciting."

Customer Service Representative

"It's nothing like college—I can't get away with generalities and 'I think so's.' I have to be specific and the information I give out on the phone is relied upon for good transportation and freight decision making.

"I was a business major, and went to an employment agency to get a job. It was the first time I heard of a customer service representative. Now that I'm on the job I wish I had more math and analytical training. My job is almost all on the telephone, but some of our representatives travel and call on customers. We call on department stores, manufacturing companies, and any business that has to move merchandise and can benefit from the size of our operation and the fast service we can provide. Marketing decisions are made on the kinds of dollars spent on shipping, and so every response has to be accurate.

"I have learned how different companies with transportation needs are interrelated. I work with chemical companies, agricultural and furniture companies, all kinds of mail order and direct mail catalog companies. I may not spend my whole life at UPS, but I am getting business experience and seeing the economics of transportation make a considerable effect on profits. I am sure I can use this business experience anywhere I go."

Assistant to the President

Can a major in sociology, strong interests in art, the Third World, and politics, and experience in leading bike tours in Europe lead to a rewarding career? They did for Gail Harrity Tilney, assistant to the president of The Metropolitan Museum of Art.

"I started out with the usual job-hunting techniques, going to campus interviews, talking with friends, and checking out want ads. Nothing sounded right for me. I wanted to be an activist in the Third World, having something to do with economic development. I wanted to be in Washington and *do* something that mattered. While visiting a friend in Washington, I realized I had an affiliation with three United States senators for possible job connections: first from the state where my parents lived, second from the state where I went to college, and third from the state where my family had a summer place. Starting out cold, I rapped on each door asking for work after a friend advised me to say that I would take anything, even typing. For a feminist, that wasn't easy! Luck played a big part in finding that first job within two hours of my search.

"I worked in a senatorial office for four years, teaching art on Saturdays, and spending each summer organizing and leading teenage bike trips through Europe. I left my senatorial job, deciding to pursue my Third World interest in a year of travel in the Mideast, Far East, and Asia. After my year abroad and one more year in my Washington job, I combined my senatorial and travel experience to spend two years as a lobbyist for a travel agents' association. At this time I became aware that in order to develop the kind of career I wanted in Washington I would have to go to law school, establish a residence and run for elected office. I decided against the election route and instead followed my two older brothers to business school, getting an MBA from Yale.

"Still interested in economic development in the Third World, two other business school students and I established a business consultation group in a refugee camp in Somalia, Africa, during the summer vacation. Back at Yale for my final MBA year, and concentrating on my art interest, I took a part-time consulting job for New York's Metropolitan Museum in the spring. As a result of my part-time experience, I was offered a full-time job as manager of purchasing when I graduated.

"Purchasing in a nonprofit institution like the Metropolitan is different because you don't have to purchase the same materials over and over again on a planned budget. For example, if the conservation department needs the latest piece of microscopic equipment, they may not need another one for 20 years. Figuring out how to finance the purchase is part of the job. A purchaser in a nonprofit organization must be very creative; entrepreneurial skills are needed. Cutting major costs without cutting service and quality of programs at the Met is the mission of this job.

"I was manager of purchasing for two-and-a-half years before being promoted to the assistant to the president, where I've been for six months. I love bringing my business skills to a nonprofit institution and want to point out to college students to remember that many interesting jobs in the world are in companies that can't afford to recruit on your campus. Think about the environment you want to be in, and don't wait for the company to come to you. Reach out to the kinds of places and experiences that you want to try out, no matter where they are, as you send out your résumés and line up your interviews."

Fund-raiser

"I manage a campaign to raise a particular sum of money for corporations, churches, public interest groups, colleges, and numbers of nonprofit organizations (businesses organized for purposes other than making a profit—for example, to provide a service, such as public service broadcasting). My day begins early and goes until at least 10 at night when I am in the middle of a big project. I work on long-term, goal-oriented plans to generate givers. I do everything from putting together the brochures, to having videos made, and planning and hosting dinner and wine and cheese parties. On my last six-month project, I had about 70 meetings and spoke to over 600 people.

"I travel for my company, but most jobs are within commuting distance. I work for months at a time, and when the campaign is over, I take some time off before starting the next one. Our fund-raising firm gives us all a chance to select the types of jobs we like and are good at. We also vary the long-term year projects with short special events fund-raising projects for the local fine arts museum or public library.

"Fund-raising is a public relations and consulting job. After a few years as a fund-raiser, the skills developed can get you into many related business areas, but most of my friends have stayed in fund-raising or have gone to a PR firm. What I like about this job is the mix of organizations we work for and the work we do to keep public institutions and public interest issues funded."

Management Consultant

"There are three phases in being a management consultant. The first, 'grinder,' is for the beginner right out of business school who does all the legwork, research, and analysis for the project. Management consulting is a team effort. You work with other consultants within your own firm to solve problems for your client, and you work with the client's management staff as well.

"After I'd proven myself with the research questions, I got to the second step, the 'minder' phase. That's designing and developing week-long seminars for middle and senior managers of my client, presenting the research and perspectives to them. The last phase, the 'finder' stage, will happen when I have been here long enough to initiate new clients, to establish a good enough relationship with my present clients so they will come back for more consulting. Our successful consultants develop long-term clients that will call on our firm whenever they have a problem to be solved by outside management consultants. If you're good at this, you move right along the three phases, taking more and more responsibility for influencing the client with your solutions. If you are not so good, you stay in the grinder phase doing the research part, and if you stay too long, you move on to another career. It takes most of us less than two years to be well into the second, 'minder,' phase, where we are given opportunities to meet more and more clients that we can persuade to come back for more."

Publicist

"A publicist has to know the truth and tell it. I work for a publicity firm in New York City that specializes in radio and television interviews for authors and book publishers. Our firm knows everyone on radio, in the newspaper field, and on television all around the country, no matter how small the market. In order for interviewers to trust us, we always tell them if the guest is great, or if he is just a little great. We may say, 'Your viewers will love this issue, but the book is better than the author so just spend two minutes speaking to the author and focus in on her book for the rest of the time.' Or when he is super, I say, 'Forget the book, your listeners will really get a kick out of listening to this author!'

"Organization and detail are the keys to a successful record with broadcasters and clients. We have memos within memos of time, place, and event. We are careful about our changes and confirmations for all of our placements with the broadcasting stations. It's an exciting job because there are new books out every day. We seldom work with the same author for more than a few months, then it's on to other issues and new people. The tough part is when you're sure you've got Johnny Carson, Merv Griffin, or Donahue all sold on a particular author, and then you hear that you've lost it—a change has been made and all of that planned work goes down the tube. It's even worse when you get your client on a national broadcast, the preceding interview runs over, and your client never gets on stage! Those are the hard parts. The fun and exciting part is when you push someone that everyone is wary about and WOW! a bestselling author is on her way and you're in on it from the beginning."

Athletic Trainer

"I am a certified athletic trainer at Illinois State University and I have always loved sports and wanted to be around jocks. I supervise athletic training for 16 intercollegiate sports. My job is divided into two areas—prevention and rehabilitation. I do a lot of prevention taping; in fact, sprained ankles are the most common sports injury. But just as important for prevention, I check equipment and supervise the strength and conditioning programs of every workout.

"On the rehabilitation side, we are the first on the field for the injured athlete. Healing requires ice, heat, whirlpool baths, elastic bandages, and sometimes massage. I also treat many students who play sports on their own and get injuries. I help them with tennis elbow, stiff neck, ankle and knee problems from skiing, climbing, and biking. I am proud of the service we give. We have the proper training and equipment and provide good care for all of our students who need prevention and rehab the athletic injuries. I wouldn't be anywhere else—the world of sports is a team effort, and I love being part of that team."

Intelligence Officer

"James Bond has always been my hero. I was easily recruited right out of college for an intelligence job with the top dog of intelligence—the CIA. An English lit major, I now work for the CIA's newspaper, *National Intelligence Daily,* an up-to-the-minute report of happenings around the world distributed daily to top U.S. policy makers.

"Intelligence means information needed or desired by the government. It includes the process of getting the raw information, evaluating it, protecting and eventually exploiting the information. Intelligence is knowledge, organization, and process. The process begins with collecting the information.

"I was given routine newspaper assignments when I first joined the CIA. However, my security clearance for the job was *not* routine. I began researching articles for other reporters to write until I finally earned a writing assignment of my own. My last assignment was to research and write biographical data on members of the Soviet Politburo.

"Even though the pay is low to start with (GS-7, which paid $17,824 in 1985), it's an exciting job and I like being in Virginia at the CIA headquarters. Unlike many stereotypes I had heard of the CIA, there are as many liberal arts people around here as there are military and hi-tech types!"

PART
3

CAREER GROUPS

ART, ARCHITECTURE, AND DESIGN

ABOUT THESE CAREERS

Creativity and the ability to communicate, along with luck and drive, are necessary to succeed in this career group, which represents about a million jobs.

Even in the best of times, the number of performing artists always exceeds the number of job openings. The difficulty of earning a living as a performer is one reason why many artists earn their living through teaching or routine jobs, such as waiting on tables and word processing. They take on unrelated jobs that will support them while they study and audition for performing arts work, and during the many, many times between jobs.

Evening work is a regular part of the performing artist's life. Rehearsals may be held late at night and on weekends and holidays. When performances are given on the road, weekend traveling is often necessary. Travel, irregular hours, and unemployment are all very hard on family and social life.

A college degree counts less in the performing arts than in many other careers. More important to artists are the professional schools of acting, dance, and music, many of which are located in the major cities where the work opportunities also exist. A professional school whose goal is to turn out the top musician, or actor, or dancer is the best place for your training. In order to find a professional school, write to the professional association at the end of the particular career description that interests you and ask for a list of approved schools.

Architects and designers spend long hours at the drawing board in well-equipped offices. New graduates usually begin as junior drafters in architectural firms, where they are closely supervised. Until junior members of a firm have gained experience and paid their "professional beginner's dues," they are often asked to work overtime to meet deadlines and to do the routine, tedious work that experienced architects prefer not to do.

Camera operators, like news photographers, advance as their work becomes known and they build a reputation. Camera operators can become directors of photography for movies and TV programs.

Architecture education requires a four- or five-year program. Commercial art, interior design, and photography require a two- or three-year professional or specialty school.

PERFORMING ARTS

ACTOR OR ACTRESS

Entertains people through performances on the stage, film, and television

What's It Like To Be an Actor or Actress?

Making a character come to life on stage or film is a glamour job that attracts many talented young people each year. Most actors and actresses struggle for a start in acting and pick up parts wherever they can—often as volunteers in community, church, and school theater groups where they hope they will be seen and reviewed. The frustrating parts of being in a glamour career are the lack of money, the limited number of "big breaks," not knowing when or where the next job will come from, losing a good acting job because you are an inch too tall or too short, and constantly having to lay yourself on the line for auditions. "However," says Porter Anderson, a graduate student in theater at Ohio State, "if the love for the art is there, all of the work seems worth the trouble. It is simply the only thing to do."

What Education and Skills Will I Need?

High school: College preparatory courses and as much acting experience as possible.

College: A theater arts or drama major offers experience in school productions. Working in summer stock is also useful. Acting experience is more important than the number of years in college. Experience in your community can be the best way to become recognized as you build your acting record for future recommendations.

Computer skills: Skill level 3—READ, ENTER, PRINT. It helps if an actor has word processing skills in order to do the necessary paperwork required of job hunting. Most actors are constantly looking for acting work plus jobs to earn their daily living while waiting for acting work. That means they are always sending out résumés and cover letters.

Personal skills: Acting demands patience, physical stamina, and total commitment, since aspiring actors and actresses must wait for parts or filming schedules, work long hours, and travel often. Evening work is a regular part of a stage actor's life.

How Many Actors Are There and Where Do They Work?

There are 34,000 actors and actresses working in stage plays, films (including TV films), industrial shows, and commercials. Many others are between acting jobs, so the total number is actually much higher. In the winter, most job opportunities on the stage are in New York. In the summer, stock companies in suburban and resort areas provide employment, although most casts are selected in New York City. Film employment is centered in Hollywood and New York.

How Much Money Will I Make?

Professional actors belong to unions. In 1984, the minimum salary for a Broadway actor was $700 a week. Off-Broadway paid from $200 to $420 a week. Motion pictures offered a minimum of $361 a day to actors and $87 a day to extras. Most actors get little if any unemployment insurance, since they seldom have enough employment in any state to meet the eligibility requirements. The Screen Actors Guild, which has over 40,000 members, reports that 20,000 members had *no* earnings, and 27,000 members earned less than $6,000 in a recent year. Only 6 percent earned over $25,000 and 650 members out of the 40,000 earned over $35,000. Therefore, most actors and actresses supplement their incomes from acting with income from other jobs.

What Are the Job Opportunities?

Earning a living as an actor is often nearly impossible and almost always difficult. New York City is flooded with young, talented, well-trained people looking desperately for the few jobs available. The best places to look are commercial theaters, non-profit acting companies, and television.

Related Careers

Dancer   Radio and TV announcer
Disc jockey   Stage manager
Drama teacher

Where Can I Get More Information?

American Theatre Association
1010 Wisconsin Avenue, NW
Washington, D.C. 20007

The American National Theater and Academy (ANTA)
245 West 52nd Street
New York, New York 10019

ANTA is an organization for actors looking for a placement service in New York City, for advice on how to select an agent, and for a list of producers. It is a good place to begin to learn about the job system in the theater.

DANCER

Expresses ideas and emotions through body movements

What's It Like To Be a Dancer?

Most dancers work together as a chorus in dance productions for the stage, movies, and television. Some are selected for special dance numbers, and a small number of top artists do solo work. The few dancers who become choreographers create new ballets or dance routines. Others become dance directors who train dancers in new productions. Teachers usually teach in a professional dancing school or teach dance courses in colleges and universities.

Stephen Wynne, a 19-year-old scholarship dancer in the American Ballet Theatre of New York City, says, "Seek out a reputable dance school, one associated with a company. Or ask a professional ballet dancer to recommend a good school. Get several opinions. Take as many classes as you can, as soon as you can, to get in shape. And most importantly—don't wait! If you aren't sure you want to be a dancer, you *will* be after a week or so in ballet school. The only part of being a ballet dancer that I don't like," explains Wynne, "is the dieting. I don't like to diet. Some dancers don't have to, but diet or no diet, we must all stay away from junk foods. The best part of dancing is the noticeable improvement—being able to do things today you couldn't do the day before. I like the excitement of controlling movement and the viewers' appreciation. I also love the discipline that dancing demands. In other words, the best thing about dancing is dancing!"

The only thing that Janine Ceballos, a ballet dancer just chosen for a Belgian dance company wants to add is, "I like working closely with a teacher, relating to him or her and listening to the music. I love dancers. They are nutty people, but interesting!"

What Education and Skills Will I Need?

Professional training: Performers begin their training at the age of 7 for ballet and by 12 or younger for other kinds of dance.

Professional training includes 10 to 12 classes a week for 11 or 12 months a year and many hours of practice. By 17 or 18 years of age, the dancer is prepared to audition.

Professional school or high school: A good professional school is very important for the training it offers and for the connections it has for employment. In addition to dancing, students study music, literature, and history. An alternative to professional school training is a high school program that leads to a dance major in college, which is usually modern dance, and often studied within the physical education or theater arts department. This option can lead to performing or to teaching. Professional schools require teachers to be experienced performers.

Computer skills: Skill level 3—READ, ENTER, PRINT. All performers benefit by word processing skills for preparing the necessary paperwork for job hunting.

Personal skills: Dancers must have agility, coordination, grace, a sense of rhythm, and a feeling for music; also, self-discipline, patience, good body build, physical stamina, and the ability to work as part of a team.

How Many Dancers Are There and Where Do They Work?

There are about 10,000 performing dancers, and another 23,000 dance instructors in high schools, colleges, and dance schools. Performers dance mostly for theatrical producers, bands, and entertainers (36 percent). Some work in recreation services (19 percent), eating and drinking places (16 percent), and motion picture production (15 percent). About half of the dancers in major dance companies are employed in New York City. Other cities with dance companies are Los Angeles, San Francisco, Seattle, Chicago, Dallas, Houston, Salt Lake City, Cincinnati, Cleveland, Boston, Philadelphia, and Atlanta. About half of the performing dancers are women, and 85 percent of the instructors are women.

How Much Money Will I Make?

Performers belong to a union that sets their contracts and salaries. In 1984, the starting dance salary in ballet and stage production was $60 a performance. Television dancers averaged $530 a week. College dance teachers with a master's degree receive the same salary as other faculty members, usually beginning at $19,200 a year.

What Are the Job Opportunities?

Very competitive. The supply of qualified dancers far exceeds job opportunities. Excellent health and unusual physical vitality are always needed. The majority of dancers stop performing around the age of 35, although there are many exceptions in modern dance.

Related Careers

Dance therapist   Choreographer
Dance teacher   Dance critic
Recreation worker

Where Can I Get More Information?

National Dance Association
1900 Association Drive
Reston, Virginia 22091

Ballet Society, New York State Theater
1865 Broadway
New York, New York 10023

American Dance Guild
570 Seventh Avenue, 20th floor
New York, New York 10018

MUSICIAN

Expresses ideas and emotions through music

What's It Like To Be a Musician?

Popular professional musicians play in concerts, dance bands in nightclubs, restaurants, and at special parties. The best known bands, rock groups, jazz groups, and solo performers often give concerts and perform on television. Classical musicians play in symphony, opera, and theater orchestras, and in chamber groups. Harpsichordist Martin Pearlman studied music at Cornell. He went on for a graduate degree in composition at Yale, and then went to Europe for his principal harpsichord studies. Upon his return, he founded the Boston-based *Blanchetto Musicale*, a Baroque orchestra performing on period instruments. His successful group gives annual subscription performances in Boston, goes on tours, and makes records. Pearlman has turned a love for his instrument into a fulfilling career that everyone had told him "couldn't be done."

What Education and Skills Will I Need?

Professional training: Professional musicians usually begin their training at an early age in elementary school with intensive study in private lessons. They audition for symphony orchestras, chamber groups, and other professional groups whenever they are ready.

High school: Preparation for college with as much music experience as possible. Many high school students choose their college by the quality of instruction it offers in their particular instrument. Many popular musicians do not have a college degree.

College: There are about 500 colleges, universities, and music conservatories that offer training in musical performance, history, and theory. There are an additional 100 that offer music education.

Computer skills: Skill level 3—READ, ENTER, PRINT. Performing artists have more time for practicing and less for job hunting if they have word processing skills.

Personal skills: Self-discipline, talent, versatility, creative ability, and stage presence are necessary for success.

How Many Musicians Are There and Where Do They Work?

There are 192,000 employed musicians; most of them work for theater producers, bands, and entertainers (36 percent), many others work for churches (30 percent), and still others work for eating and drinking places (21 percent). The majority of the musicians work in New York, Chicago, Los Angeles, Nashville, Miami Beach, and New Orleans. Classical musicians perform with one of the 30 major symphony groups, the 37 regional orchestras, the 95 metropolitan orchestras, and hundreds of smaller groups.

How Much Money Will I Make?

Musicians belong to the American Federation of Musicians (AFL-CIO), and concert soloists belong to the American Guild of Musical Artists. In 1984, major symphony orchestra musicians earned from $331 to $778 a week. Music teachers received the same as other teachers in their school systems.

What Are the Job Opportunities?

All music jobs are extremely competitive. There are many more talented musicians of all kinds—classical, pop, teachers, and performers—than jobs.

Related Careers

Arranger
Composer
Copyist
Music teacher

Music therapist
Music salesperson
Radio and TV music
    producer
Disc jockey

Where Can I Get More Information?

American Federation of Musicians
1500 Broadway
New York, New York 10036

National Association of Schools of Music
11250 Roger Bacon Drive
Reston, Virginia 22090

SINGER

Interprets music through voice production, melody, and harmony

What's It Like To Be a Singer?

Singers are classified by the type of music they sing, such as opera, rock, folk, or country and western, or according to their voice range—soprano, contralto, tenor, baritone, or bass. "It takes experience and exposure to 'make it' in a singing career," says, Linda Smyth, who at 38 is an understudy at the New York City Opera Company. "Holding out for star roles in opera means you understudy rather than sing in the chorus. It's necessary to take many jobs, hopefully in music, to pay my way until I get that audition acceptance to star in the company. I love singing and have the discipline for exercise, vocalizing, and studying roles, diction, and style. Music is what I want to do."

What Education and Skills Will I Need?

Professional training: Voice training does not begin until after you have matured physically. It continues for years after a singer's professional career has started.

High school: Dance and piano are often an asset to getting a singing job; working on these skills and preparing for a music career by studying music theory is helpful.

College: About 500 colleges and conservatories offer degrees in music. Popular singers often get started in their careers by performing in local college and community shows or restaurants.

How Many Singers Are There and Where Do They Work?

There are 21,000 employed singers; 53 percent work for theatrical producers, bands, and entertainers, and 15 percent work in eating and drinking places. Many others are between jobs. Most of the singing jobs are in New York, Los Angeles, Las Vegas, San Francisco, Dallas, and Chicago. Nashville is the major center for country and western singers. In addition, there are singers all over the country working part time in church and synagogue choirs, in local restaurants and bars, and giving private singing lessons.

How Much Money Will I Make?

The union minimum for concert singers in a chorus was $65 per performance in 1984. Opera members earned slightly less per performance. Like other performing artists, most singers have a hard time earning enough to live on because their jobs are so irregular.

What Are the Job Opportunities?

Like all the performing arts, singing jobs are very competitive, regardless of the economy. There are always more talented, hard-working, ambitious singers than there are jobs.

Related Careers

Composer	Arranger
Songwriter	Choir director
Music teacher	Music salesperson
Music technician	Music librarian

Where Can I Get More Information?

American Federation of Musicians
1500 Broadway
New York, New York 10036

National Association of Schools of Music
11250 Roger Bacon Drive
Reston, Virginia 22090

ARCHITECTURE

ARCHITECT

Plans and designs buildings and other structures

What's It Like To Be an Architect?

Architect's meet and discuss with clients the purpose, costs, preferences for style, and plan of structures to be built. They consider the local building and zoning laws and make the primary drawings of the building to show the client. The final design is a working one, including details of the plumbing, electrical, and heating systems. Architects help their clients select a building contractor and continue to represent the client until the structure is completed and all tests are made. Self-employed architects work on a variety of projects from homes, churches, and office buildings, to renewal projects, college campuses, new towns, and urban planning. When working for large architectural firms, architects often specialize in one phase of the work, such as design or construction contracts. This frequently requires working with engineers, city planners, and landscape architects.

Architect Jonathan Felsman was a political science major in college. After a year with VISTA on a city planning project, Felsman took a two-year master's in architecture, returning to his hometown of Philadelphia to work at several different jobs, including designing free playground spaces in the city. His filmmaker wife needed to be in New York City for her career, so Felsman pounded the pavement, talked to his friends, and landed his first New York job designing skyscrapers. He stayed in that job for three years and, after one more job change, Jonathan is now happy working for an architectural and planning firm with offices at the top of New York's Chrysler Building. He designs townhouses and office buildings and is into development of real estate properties. He loves his work because he gets to begin and complete a whole project. When he and a coworker start a project, they spend about six months at the drawing board and then continue working on the same project another year and a half until the building is complete. Jonathan says that many architects work in large groups on one project, each person specializing and doing a small part of each job. What he likes is the opportunity to work on the details of his plans, and the control he has over the complete assignment.

What Education and Skills Will I Need?

High school: Preparation for college, with an emphasis on mathematics, physics, and art.

College: Felsman wants students to be aware that any major can take you into architecture. There are two basic programs: one is the five-year plan in which you start as a freshman, and the other, which Felsman chose, is the six-year plan designed for liberal arts graduates with a two-year master's degree. There are 92 accredited schools of architecture offering a five-year bachelor's of architecture degree or a six-year program for a master's of architecture degree. After three years of experience, an architect takes a state examination for a license to practice.

Computer skills: Skill level 6—READ, ENTER, PRINT, SELECT, GRAPHICS, PROGRAM PROFICIENCY. Most architects use computer graphics as a major tool in their work. The use of computers will be increasingly important, and many find the need for programming (level 6) as well.

Personal skills: Capacity to solve technical problems and work independently, artistic skills, computer skills, and good, competitive business abilities are necessary for architects.

How Many Architects Are There and Where Do They Work?

There are 93,000 licensed architects. About 8.5 percent are women and 3 percent are black. The great majority (71 percent) work for engineering, architectural, and surveying companies, and 6 percent work for the federal government. Most architects are employed in New York, Chicago, Los Angeles, Boston, and Washington, where many large architectural firms are located. Increasing numbers of architects are finding employment in areas of the South and Southwest that are attracting new business and residential construction such as Dallas, Fort Worth, Phoenix, and a number of Florida cities.

How Much Money Will I Make?

The median salary for all architects in 1984 was $28,600—most earning between $20,000 and $37,000. The top 10 percent make over $40,000.

What Are the Job Opportunities?

This is a very competitive field in which there are more graduates than jobs. The demand for architects is highly dependent upon the economy.

Related Careers

Civil engineer
Urban planner
Industrial designer

Building contractor
Landscape architect

Where Can I Get More Information?

The American Institute of Architects
1735 New York Avenue, NW
Washington, D.C. 20006

DESIGN

GRAPHIC ARTIST

Creates the artwork for publications, films, textiles, greeting cards, and industrial products

What's It Like To Be a Graphic Artist?

Most people in the field work in either illustration or design. Illustrators paint, draw, or use computers to create pictures.

The major specialities are fashion artists, medical and scientific illustrators, cartoonists, and animators. Designers create or supervise the visual images of advertisements and industrial products. An *art director* is an art and design specialist who assigns work to illustrators and designers and decides the art, design, photography, and type style that go into published materials and TV advertisements. *Computer graphics* is the newest method for creating artwork. In place of paint brushes, pens and pencils, photographs, matting knives, glue, artboards, and overlays, the computer graphics artist uses the computer screen to create images of uniform and irregular shapes, change colors, choose the size of an image, scale, rotate, duplicate, and move and erase objects, of all which can be done faster by computer than by hand. Because computer graphics are so new, most graphic artists learn the computer skills on the job. Nelson Johnston, a graphic artist who learned on the job, says that the common questions and concerns of artists who are training on computers are these: "Will I be able to operate this device? Does this mean that everything I do will be created by computer? Will I have to go back to school? Will I be so caught up in this computer and keyboard that I won't be able to think creatively anymore?" Nelson points out that for the artist, these are computer-anxiety questions, and after a very few hours with the computer, artists see the computer as another tool that does their job very well. Advertising graphic artist Paula Randall says she still likes to use watercolor, pen and ink, and crayons, but computers are the best way to handle 90 percent of her work in multi-image graphics.

What Education and Skills Will I Need?

High school: Preparation for an art school or a fine arts major in college. Art schools require an art aptitude test and an example of your work. Start assembling your portfolio (a collection of your best work.)

College: A two-year art school or four-year college art program will prepare you for the better commercial jobs. As in all the arts, demonstration of your ability and talent are more important than a degree.

Computer skills: Skill levels—READ, ENTER, PRINT, SELECT, GRAPHICS. If you are going to use computer graphics as a tool in your work, level 5 is basic for the rapidly increased computer use.

Personal skills: Artistic ability, imagination, a distinctive style, and the capacity to translate ideas onto paper are necessary in graphics.

How Many Graphic Artists Are There and Where Do They Work?

There are 204,000 graphic and fine artists, and about 35 percent are women. About 20 percent work in advertising, 16 percent for mailing, reproduction, and commercial art businesses, and another 16 percent work in printing and publishing. They are employed in the major cities, although New York has by far the largest concentration because it is the center of the advertising and publishing industries. Boston, Chicago, Los Angeles, and San Francisco also have many artists. Almost half of graphic artists are self-employed and work part time in order to spend the rest of their time on fine arts.

How Much Money Will I Make?

Artists in entry-level, paste-up or layout jobs often make as little as minimum wage. The median earnings for full-time graphic artists was $18,600 in 1984. Art directors, designers, and well-known freelance illustrators make from $35,000 to $45,000 a year and more.

What Are the Job Opportunities?

Chances for work and promotions will continue to be very competitive through the 1980s. Those with outstanding talent and a mastery of graphic art skills and computers will continue to be in demand in spite of the competition.

Related Careers

Industrial designer
Interior designer
Photographer

Set designer
Fashion designer
Display designer

Where Can I Get More Information?

The Graphic Artists Guild
30 East 20th Street, Room 405
New York, New York 10003

American Institute of Visual Arts
1059 Third Avenue
New York, New York 10021

INDUSTRIAL DESIGNER

**Designs or arranges objects and materials
to best show off a product's appearance,
function, and value**

What's It Like To Be an Industrial Designer?

Industrial designers study their company's product and competing products to decide possibilities for change. Industrial designers develop designs for products as diverse as cars, home appliances, computers, stethoscopes, filing cabinets, fishing rods, pens, and piggy banks. They combine artistic talent with research on product use, marketing, materials, and production methods to create the most appealing design for competition in the marketplace. Josie Erickson wanted to have an art career, but because there are so few women in it, she never thought of industrial design until her art professor suggested it as an alternative to the overcrowded art field. She tells what her job in a manufacturing company outside Chicago is like. "After our team selects the best design for a product, I make a model of it, often of clay so that it can be easily modified. After any necessary revisions, I make a working model, usually of the material to be used in the finished product. The approved model then is put into production. When I learned that all industrial designers experience the frustration of having many designs rejected, I began to find my job a real challenge. I like working with the team, and I like the business side of learning more about how to market products."

What Education and Skills Will I Need?

High school: Preparation for college, with courses in art, drafting, mathematics, and computer science.

College: Take one of the 31 college programs for industrial design that are approved by the Industrial Designers Society of America.

Computer skills: Skill level 5—READ, ENTER, PRINT, SELECT, GRAPHICS. Increased use of computer graphics makes level 5 a necessity for most jobs.

Personal skills: Creativity, artistic and drawing skills, ability to see familiar objects in new ways, ability to work with people who are not designers, and an interest in business and sales are needed for success.

How Many Industrial Designers Are There and Where Do They Work?

There are 205,000 designers, of which about 15,000 are industrial designers, one-fourth of them women. Most designers work for large manufacturing companies or for design consulting firms in New York, Chicago, Los Angeles, and San Francisco.

How Much Money Will I Make?

Designers with experience earned a median of $21,900 in 1984. The top 10 percent over $40,500.

What Are the Job Opportunities?

Jobs will be competitive as they are in all artistic professions, and the markets for new products are very dependent upon the economy each year.

Related Careers

Architect   Package designer
Graphic artist

Where Can I Get More Information?

Industrial Designers Society of America
1360 Beverly Road, Suite 303
McLean, Virginia 22101

INTERIOR DESIGNER

Plans and supervises the design and arrangement of building interiors and furnishings

What's It Like To Be an Interior Designer?

Carol Durfee is an interior designer at a Denver, Colorado, architectural firm and has a Bachelor of Fine Arts in architecture from the Rhode Island School of Design. She spends her day talking with field supervisors about space planning for current construction, and with salesworkers about new products and colors. She attends meetings with clients, visits construction sites to check progress and quality, and spends afternoons in local shops looking at draperies, carpets, and furnishings. Durfee often meets with building committees to present her plans to clients. Interior designers work closely with architects to check their plans against the blueprints and building requirements. Boston designer Michael S. Abdou, a member of the American Society of Interior Designers, says: "Your work is never duplicated—every day and every client is different. A designer is a guide who helps homeowners get the style and colors they want. Making the color schemes after you work with a client takes most of the time." Abdou is well established in his own firm, and he always takes the summers off because clients usually are not in their city homes in the summer. He advises students who like to create things "to go to the best school of art or design you can get into."

What Education and Skills Will I Need?

High school: Preparation for art school or a degree in fine arts. Begin to develop your portfolio (collection of your best artwork) while in high school.

College: Go to a three-year art school or institute of interior design, or take a degree in architecture. A college degree or a three-year professional school degree is required to be a professional member of the American Society of Interior Designers, which is necessary for the best jobs.

Computer skills: Skill level 5—READ, ENTER, PRINT, SELECT, GRAPHICS. If you use computers at all, it's as a designing tool, and therefore graphics level is necessary.

Personal skills: Artistic talent, color sense, good taste, imagination, good business judgment, and the ability to work with detail are needed to be a successful designer.

How Many Interior Designers Are There and Where Do They Work?

There are 35,000 full-time interior designers; half are men. They work for design and architectural firms in major cities. Some have their own firms; others work in department and furniture stores, for restaurant chains, and home furnishings magazines.

How Much Money Will I Make?

The median salary for experienced designers was $21,900 in 1984. The top 10 percent made over $40,500 a year.

What Are the Job Opportunities?

Jobs are competitive. The slower the economy and home construction market, the more difficult it is to find full-time employment.

Related Careers

Set designer   Floral designer
Fashion designer   Fabric designer

Where Can I Get More Information?

American Society of Interior Designers
1430 Broadway
New York, New York 10018

PHOTOGRAPHER OR CAMERA OPERATOR

**Uses cameras and film to portray people,
places, and events**

What's It Like To Be a Photographer or Camera Operator?

As a writer uses words, a photographer uses a camera to take pictures for artistic or technical purposes, such as portrait photography, commercial photography, television entertainment and news, or photojournalism. Some specialize in scientific, medical, or engineering photography, and their pictures enable thousands of people to see a world normally hidden from view. Others specialize in portraits, commercial photography, industrial work, or photojournalism. Photojournalism combines photographic ability with news reporting. Most photographers own several different cameras, depending on their specialty. Camera operators film news events, television shows, movies, commercials, and cartoons. They often film directly on video which is then transmitted by satellite to their television newscasting station for instant viewing on TV.

John and Rosanna Nelson have been in partnership in a photographic portrait business for thirty years in a small city. They have two galleries in neighboring suburbs and are successful because they work long hours and have always been careful in their work. The Nelsons want students to know that "if you are going into the photography business, you will need to know about business management, how to relax people, and how to promote your business as much as how to use the camera. Photography has come of age in the last fifteen years, with technology and materials enabling more creative work. With the tools available, there's no limitation on creativity."

What Education and Skills Will I Need?

High school: Take art courses along with college preparation.
College: Education required varies from on-the-job training to courses leading to a degree in photography. The future belongs to the photographer whose training and experience enables her or him to do more than other photographers can do. Preparation for a career in photography must include knowledge of the field in which photography is to be applied. Economics, geography, international affairs, and journalism are important fields for the photojournalist. A career in advertising photography requires knowledge of art and design and some background in advertising.
Computer skills: Skill level 3—READ, ENTER, PRINT. If any technical processing is needed, specialized monitors require the photographer to READ instructions for processing. Color scanning and enlarging controlled by computers require level 3.
Personal skills: Photographers need good eyesight, artistic ability, and manual dexterity. News photographers need the ability to see the potential for a good photo in a situation and to act quickly; portrait photographers need the ability to help people relax. Original ideas are necessary for success in freelance work.

How Many Photographers and Camera Operators Are There and Where Do They Work?

There are 101,000 photographers and camera operators; 23 percent are women, and 5 percent are black. They work in portrait studios (26 percent), for the government (11 percent), commercial art firms (11 percent), printers and publishers (11 percent), and for educational services (9 percent).

How Much Money Will I Make?

The median income for photographers was $17,400 a year in 1984. Camera operators made slightly more. Newspaper union rates averaged $285 to $450 a week. Portrait photographers in business for themselves and with a national reputation earn much more. The top magazine photographers with a national reputation earn over $75,000 a year. Most, however, work very hard in an office in their home for incomes between $21,000 and $26,000 a year.

What Are the Job Opportunities?

Portrait photography is a very competitive business. The newspaper, business and industry, law enforcement, and scientific fields are expected to need more photographers. Well-trained people with strong technical backgrounds will have the best opportunities. Camera operator jobs will continue to be very competitive through the 1980s.

Related Careers

Graphic artist   Painter
Illustrator

Where Can I Get More Information?

Professional Photographers of America
1090 Executive Way
Des Plaines, Illinois 60018

American Society of Magazine Photographers
205 Lexington Avenue
New York, New York 10016

AVIATION

ABOUT THESE CAREERS

Pilots make more money with less required academic education than any other job in the country. Even though airline pilots are usually college graduates, many of them get their flight training in the military. Air traffic controllers come from many college backgrounds; flight attendants usually have two years of college.

In aviation, jobs involve shift work around the clock. Air traffic controllers work a basic 40-hour week; however, they are assigned to night shifts on a rotating basis. Air traffic controllers work under great stress. They must keep track of several planes at the same time and make certain all pilots receive correct instructions.

Pilots work 100 hours a month, but because their schedules are irregular, some actually fly 30 hours while others may fly 90 hours a month. Although flying does not involve much physical effort, the pilot is often subject to mental stress and must be constantly alert and prepared to make decisions quickly.

Flight attendants have the opportunity to meet interesting people and to see new places. However, the work can be strenuous and trying. Attendants stand during much of the flight and must remain pleasant and efficient, regardless of how tired from jet lag they may be.

Advancement in aviation is usually very clearly determined. Seniority is established by union contracts. After 5 to 10 years, flight engineers advance on the basis of seniority to copilots, who are in charge of aircraft scheduling and flight procedures. Advancement for all pilots is generally limited to other flying jobs. Advancement opportunities for flight attendants are very limited.

Aviation changed drastically in 1985, when government deregulation led to expansion within the industry, causing a great need for more pilots and other aviation personnel. The demand for pilots is so great that many of the age and flight-hour requirements have been dropped in order to get the numbers needed. And for every pilot hired in 1985, two flight attendants have been hired. Aviation has become a hot career in the late eighties.

AIRLINE PILOT

Flies planes to transport passengers and cargo, to dust crops, to inspect powerlines and other situations, and to take aerial photographs

What's It Like To Be a Pilot?

The pilot, referred to as the captain or first officer of the plane, operates the controls and performs other necessary tasks for flying the plane, keeping it on course, and landing it safely. The flight engineer is third in line to pilot. The flight engineer monitors the operation of the different mechanical and electrical devices aboard the plane. He or she helps the pilot and copilot make preflight checks of instruments and equipment and watches these checks during the flight. Airlines are just beginning to hire women flight engineers.

First Officer Charles T. Huggins, Jr., Eastern Airlines, advises young people to get a college education because airlines have not hired pilots without college degrees since the 1970s. "Then," says Huggins, "get plenty of experience. That means the military. Even though it's a five- or six-year obligation for pilots, the flying experience in the military is unparalleled by anything else. My daily activity includes jogging and exercising because the length of a pilot's career depends upon taking care of his health, that is, how long he can hold a Federal Aviation Administration medical certificate." Huggins has two children and is expecting a third. He says that "a person unable to adjust to a job in which he or she is not home every day would not like it." When his 15 work days per month are over, the rest of his time is spent with his family.

What Education and Skills Will I Need?

High school: Preparation for college, or technical school, or the military.

College: Most pilots are college graduates and have traditionally been trained through the United States military service. Since the Vietnam War has ended and the demand for pilots has increased in the newly deregulated aviation industry, a much larger percentage of pilots have been trained through flying schools. Flight engineers have been hired after 500 hours of flying time since the shortage began in 1985. It takes 250 hours of flight time to get a commercial license. Most airlines hire flight engineers who are licensed as commercial pilots. Flight engineers work their way to copilot and then to pilot. Pilots must be at least 23 years old and can fly as long as they can pass the required physical examination.

Computer skills: Skill level 2—READ, ENTER. Most schedules are displayed on monitors, and often pilots must enter flight information.

Personal skills: Decision making and accurate judgment under pressure are required of pilots.

How Many Pilots Are There and Where Do They Work?

There are 80,000 pilots; 4 percent are women and 1 percent are black. Three-fifths work for scheduled airlines, and the others work as flight instructors, for business firms, for agriculture projects, or for the government.

How Much Money Will I Make?

Captains and copilots are among the highest paid wage earners in the country. In 1985, the top pilot pay went to a senior pilot of a Boeing 747 at Flying Tigers airlines, a cargo carrier; he earned $174,000 a year. On the other hand, a senior captain piloting a small, twin-engine BAC 111 for Florida Express made $36,000 a year. Average pay for a senior captain is $80,000, and captains for nonunion airlines and for corporations get much less. Average salary for a corporate pilot is $40,000 to $56,000, and $30,000 to $40,000 for a copilot. A beginning flight engineer can start as low as $1,000 a month, but makes $3,000 a month within a year. Flight engineers start at an average of $16,000.

What Are the Job Opportunities?

They're soaring! The number of pilots hired went from 800 in 1984 to 8,000 in 1985. It's a record need for the aviation industry. More and more pilots in their 40s and 50s, without a college degree, and wearing glasses are being hired. The opportunities in aviation have increased in every job in the industry since the 1985 deregulation. The growth of People Express is a good example of the skyrocketing growth of aviation in America in the late eighties. If you like it, the sky's the limit!

Related Careers

Helicopter pilot   Air traffic controller

Where Can I Get More Information?

Airline Pilots Association
1625 Massachusetts Avenue, NW
Washington, D.C. 20036

AIR TRAFFIC CONTROLLER

Keeps track of planes flying within an assigned area and gives pilots instructions that keep planes separated

What's It Like To Be an Air Traffic Controller?

Air traffic controllers are number one on the burnout list. They have a more stressful job than anyone else. Their immediate concern is safety, but they also must direct planes efficiently to minimize delays. Some regulate airport traffic; others regulate flights between airports. Relying both on radar and visual observation, they closely monitor each lane and maintain a safe distance between all aircraft while guiding pilots between the hangar or ramp and the end of the airport's airspace. Air traffic controllers work in a tower near the runway to keep track of planes that are on the ground and in the air nearby. They radio pilots to give them permission to taxi, take off, or land. They must keep track of many planes at once. Controllers notify enroute controllers to watch the plane after take off. Each enroute controller is responsible for a certain airspace. For instance, one controller may be responsible for all planes that are 30 to 100 miles north of the airport and flying between 6,000 and 8,000 feet. All commercial planes are under the responsibility of an air traffic controller at all times.

What Education and Skills Will I Need?

High school: Preparation for technical, community, or four-year college.

College: Most air traffic controllers have four years of college before taking the federal civil service exam and training program at the Federal Aviation Administration (FAA) Academy in Oklahoma City. After they are selected, controllers are trained on the job. It takes two to three years to become fully qualified. Others have learned in the military.

Computer skills: Skill level 2—READ, ENTER. Many work with computer terminals and enter information about planes.
Personal skills: Speech skills must be perfect and vision correctable to 20–20. A physical exam is necessary every year for this crucial job in air safety. A stable temperament and good judgment are also required.

How Many Air Traffic Controllers Are There and Where Do They Work?

There are 22,000 air traffic controllers. They all work for the federal government (FAA). Most work at the major airports or at air-route traffic control centers near large cities.

How Much Money Will I Make?

In 1985, the starting salary for air traffic controller trainees was $17,800 a year. The average salary for experienced controllers was $35,400 a year.

What Are the Job Opportunities?

Excellent. The growing aviation industry, technology that isn't keeping up with that growth, and burnout on the job result in a demand for more traffic controllers than are available.

Related Careers

Airline radio operator   Airplane dispatcher
Flight service specialist

Where Can I Get More Information?

Dial the toll-free number 1–800–555–1212 for United States Civil Service Commission Job Information and ask for the number of the nearest Civil Service Job Information Center, or check your local phone book.

FLIGHT ATTENDANT

**Makes the airline passengers' flight safe,
comfortable, and enjoyable**

What's It Like To Be a Flight Attendant?

Before each flight, flight attendants check supplies, food, beverages, and emergency gear in the plane's cabin. They greet the passengers, check their tickets, and help with coats and luggage, small children, and babies. During the flight they give safety instructions and serve beverages and precooked meals. T. Q. Pham, a flight attendant with Eastern Airlines, flies 80 hours a month with 35 hours of groundwork duties. He points out to newcomers that all airline jobs with passenger contact have some required shift work. Because airlines run flights 365 days a year, 24 hours a day, they require their personnel to take turns with this schedule. Planes carry 1 to 10 flight attendants, while 747 jetliners carry as many as 16 attendants. Pham says that what he likes best about his work is the amount of travel and time off compared to other jobs.

What Education and Skills Will I Need?

High school: Preparation for community, business, or four-year college.

College: At least two years of college are required by major airlines. The ability to speak a foreign language fluently is essential to be an attendant on an international route.

Physical qualifications: You must be in excellent health, with good voice and vision. You must be at least 19 years old. Even though airlines specify physical attractiveness, you don't have to be "tall, dark, and handsome," or a "beauty queen" to be a flight attendant!

Computer skills: Skill level 2—READ, ENTER. These are the basics needed in order to read the terminal and enter passenger information.

Personal skills: Poise, tact, and resourcefulness are needed in this work to be helpful to all passengers and reassuring to the many customers who often are afraid of flying.

How Many Flight Attendants Are There and Where Do They Work?

There are 64,000 flight attendants, 84 percent are women, 16 percent are men, and 11 percent are black. They work for scheduled airlines, usually headquartered near large cities where most airlines fly.

How Much Money Will I Make?

In 1984, the union contracts set the minimum salary of beginning flight attendants at an average of $13,000 a year. The major airlines paid an average of $23,000 a year to attendants with experience. Reduced airfare for attendants and their families is an additional benefit of the job.

What Are the Job Opportunities?

Great opportunities! Since the skyrocketing growth of the aviation industry when the government deregulated controls, 1,300 flight attendants were hired in 1985. Some college is required. If you speak Spanish, French, or German, you will improve your salary.

Related Careers

Tour guide   Reservations agent
Social director

Where Can I Get More Information?

For specific information about qualifications and jobs, write to the particular airlines that interest you. Keep in mind that local and regional airlines may have good opportunities and be less competitive than the national airlines. Beware of "air attendant schools," as the airlines will give you their own training after you are hired.

BUSINESS: ADMINISTRATION AND MANAGEMENT

ABOUT THESE CAREERS

Managers make a lot of money. There are 10 million of them in America. The president of Chrysler, Mom and Pop at the corner store, the local postmaster, the manager of the private tennis club, the local branch manager, and the chief executive officer of the city hospital are all managers. They plan, organize, direct, and control the major functions of their organizations.

The competition is stiff for getting into a management training program in a major corporation, even with a college degree. A Master of Business Administration (MBA) is your best bet for the top management programs. People in business have varied college backgrounds. Many are from liberal arts programs, with majors in economics, accounting, statistics, and law. A law degree or CPA is a good way to beat the competition of the traditional MBAs. Management is not an entry-level job. Teachers become principals, doctors and nurses become hospital administrators, salespeople become managers, and bank tellers become branch managers.

During the 1980s there has been an upsurge in corporate educational institutes where you can learn the specific business management skills you need for advancement. You can get a master's degree at Arthur B. Little's Graduate Management Education Institute in Cambridge, Massachusetts, or a master's degree in a computer specialty at the Wang Institute. Merrill Lynch Pierce Fenner & Smith has opened its own college for stockbrokers. McDonald's Hamburger University teaches management. Both IBM and the American Telephone and Telegraph Company spend millions of dollars to educate their full-time employees in skills needed on the job as well as in management skills for advancement. When you are planning advancement through education, be sure to check the company you work for, first. You may be able to get further education at company expense instead of your own, and a company that invests in you is likely to take a strong interest in your advancement.

Working conditions vary according to the position, employer, and industry of managers. In a large corporation, a top-level manager might have a plush office and several private secretaries, whereas a production-line manager might have a simple office and use a secretarial pool. Most work long hours, some up to 80 and 90 hours a week. Some, like those in newspaper publishing, regularly work the night shift. Others, like hospital administrators, are on call 24 hours a day to deal with emergencies. And almost all managers are expected to work late when necessary.

The pace of work also varies. In the radio and television broadcasting industry, managers are subject to constant deadlines. For hotel managers, checkout time can be hectic. In retail trade businesses, seasonal changes in activity are pronounced. In the drug manufacturing industry, research projects may be long term, with schedules for completion months or even years in the future.

Managers are decision makers. The difference between managers and other workers is that they set goal policies, and work through other people to reach them.

BUSINESS MANAGER

Directs or plans the work of others in order to run a business at a profit

What's It Like To Be a Business Manager?

Business managers direct workers in sales, research, production, accounting, and purchasing. They often work in company teams to decide about sales, personnel, public relations, and how the work must be done. Directors of training programs hiring future managers for their corporations from among college graduates look for self-starters, those people who can use their initiative, who have an observing eye to see what needs to be done, who like responsibility, and who have high standards for fairness. They must be thorough, though not necessarily brilliant, and persistent to be good in their job. There are as many different management titles as there are job categories. Loan officer and branch manager are banking managers; dean and superintendent are school managers; mayor, senator are government managers; program director, public affairs director are communications managers; publisher, editor in chief are publishing managers; and plant manager, quality control manager are manufacturing managers. Reading a book such as *Iacocca: An Autobiography* will give you an idea of what it's like to be in corporate management. CEO (chief executive officer) is the personal goal of business managers. It's the top job, number one in the business. Even though the number of female MBAs is steadily increasing, the number of women in top management jobs is not at all representative of those in entry-level management. No women are on the fast track to the top management job at any Fortune 500 corporation. Even nonprofits are slow to promote women to management jobs. For example, it was not until late 1984 that The Metropolitan Museum of Art elected the first woman vice-president in the history of the museum.

What Education and Skills Will I Need?

High school: Preparation for college in whatever major that interests you, taking as broad a program as you can do well. Participate in extracurricular activities that teach such management qualities as leadership, assertiveness, and sensitivity to others. Sports are especially important for learning teamwork and competitive skills that are absolutely essential in management.

College: Most executive training programs recruit liberal arts students. Ability to think and make decisions, computer skills, and an interest in a particular training program are special qualities corporations are looking for. An MBA is one good route to management, a law degree is another, a CPA still another. In addition, sales experience has always paid off in management jobs.

Computer skills: Skill level 4—READ, ENTER, PRINT, SELECT. Managers need to be able to work with spread sheets for designing budgets. Enough computer skills are necessary to play around with the figures and to ask "what if" questions.

Personal skills: Decision-making skills, assertiveness, fairness, and an interest in business are important. Self-starters and team players are what corporations are looking for.

How Many Business Managers Are There and Where Do They Work?

About 10 million salaried persons manage the nation's businesses and 2.5 million are college graduates. There are thousands more who are owners of their own businesses.

How Much Money Will I Make?

College graduates entering management trainee programs received an average of $18,000 to $21,000 a year in 1984. The median salary for managers with experience was $27,400. More than 12 percent made over $52,000. And the top managers of Fortune 500 companies take home close to or over a million dollars a year. When you think about middle-management and top-management salaries, be aware that salaries are fast becoming only a small part of what is known as the "executive compensation package," or perks. For example, a manager with a salary of $50,000 a year may get an additional $70,000 in rewards. The manager with a $200,000 salary may make as much as $580,000 more a year in bonuses, long-term incentives, fringe benefits, and perks.

What Are the Job Opportunities?

Between 1982 and 1995, 2.7 million managerial jobs will be added to the millions already in our economy as business operations become more complex. The employment of health services administrators outside hospitals is expected to increase much faster than average. Others expected to grow faster than average are bank officers, retail trade sales managers, and store managers. Those expected to grow slowly and possibly decline are secondary school administrators, postmasters, and captains of water vessels.

Related Careers

Sales manager   Money manager

Where Can I Get More Information?

The American Management Association
135 West 50th Street
New York, New York 10020

HOTEL, MOTEL, CLUB, OR RESTAURANT MANAGER

**Manages food and lodging establishments
as a profitable business, providing
maximum comfort for guests**

What's It Like To Be a Hotel, Motel, Club, or Restaurant Manager?

Hotel managers decide about room rates and credit policy, direct
the kitchen and dining rooms, and manage the housekeeping,
accounting, and maintenance departments of hotels. They are
also responsible for any problems that guests or hotel staff may
have. The job depends on the size of the hotel. Large hotels and
chains offer more specialization. A manager of a small hotel or
a self-employed hotel owner often does all of the jobs, including
front desk clerical work, advertising, and personnel.

Many opportunities for experienced managers can be found
in club and restaurant management. For instance, a country
club in Wichita, Kansas, pays its manager $75,000 a year plus
a car and other benefits.

Women have always been in the restaurant business. When
Cindy Ayres of Philadelphia was divorced, she looked for work
in the area she loved best—cooking. Starting at $60 a week, she
was up to $225 in two years, gaining experience in restaurant

cooking, menu planning, and ordering. She followed her dream and opened her own restaurant, after borrowing money from friends and the Small Business Administration for the initial investment. Now working 16 to 20 hours a day, Ayres is just where she wants to be—owner and chef of "the best new inexpensive restaurant in town."

What Education and Skills Will I Need?

High school: Preparation for college or business college. Summer work in resorts, hotels, and restaurants will help you gain experience and find out what the job is like.

College: Major in hotel administration in one of the 100 colleges offering a hotel management degree, or go to a community college, or take a correspondence course for hotel–motel management. Training programs for the large hotels look for graduates of hotel and restaurant administration. Small hotels and owner-manager lodges and restaurants do not require a degree, but they do require interest, motivation, an original idea, and capital.

Computer skills: Skill level 3—READ, ENTER, PRINT. Most hotels have computerized their reservations systems, and will teach you the necessary computer skills on the job.

Personal skills: Initiative, self-discipline, and the ability to organize and concentrate on detail are needed in food–lodging careers.

How Many Hotel, Motel, Club, or Restaurant Managers Are There and Where Do They Work?

There are 83,000 hotel and motel managers, and more than 40,000 of them are owner-managers. In addition, there are 707,000 restaurant and bar managers.

How Much Money Will I Make?

A graduate from a hotel school in a large-hotel training program starts at from $13,00 to $27,000. In 1984, hotel managers ranged from $30,000 to $80,000 a year. Ten percent made more than $47,000, often with room and board in addition to their salary.

What Are the Job Opportunities?

Chances for jobs for the college graduate who has specialized in hotel administration will be very good through the 1990s. Small lodges and restaurants in cities and resort areas are often started by young people, and even though the business is competitive, many original ideas have resulted in a comfortable income and a satisfying lifestyle for the owners.

Related Careers

Apartment manager   Sales manager
Office manager

Where Can I Get More Information?

American Hotel and Motel Association
888 Seventh Avenue
New York, New York 10019

Club Managers Association of America
7615 Winterberry Place
PO Box 34482
Washington, D.C. 20034

Council on Hotel, Restaurant, and Institutional Education
Human Development Building, Suite 5208
University Park, Pennsylvania 16802

PERSONNEL AND LABOR RELATIONS

Personnel worker: Hires and keeps the best employees available for the success of a business or government
Labor relations worker: Handles union-management relations in unionized firms

What's It Like To Be in Personnel and Labor Relations?

Personnel and labor relations workers represent management for business or government agencies, providing the link between management and employees. Personnel workers try to attract the best employees available and match them to the jobs they do best. Dealing with people is the essential activity of personnel workers. Some specialize in filling job vacancies by interviewing, selecting, and recommending applicants for job openings; some handle wage and salary administration; others specialize in training and career development on the job; and still others work in employee benefits. Lise Steg graduated from Northern Illinois University in August and found a job by mid-September. A business administration major in college, Lise worked part time getting banking experience and personnel experience in banking, which gave her an edge on the job-hunting competition. Lise tells us what it's like: "My title is *personnel records manager* for a security guard placement business that places guards in Illinois, Michigan, Wisconsin, and Indiana. They guard anything from nuclear plants to hotels. We have a great turnover of 30 to 40 a week out of 1,000 guards employed at any given time. I handle all the new hires, terminations, unemployment claims, public aid, and will eventually handle insurance and workers' compensation. I'm also going to learn the payroll and computer departments. I know there's not a lot of advancement opportunity here, but the experience is of infinite value. It's a perfect first job and I love being out of college and starting my career!"

Labor relations is not an entry-level job. People in this field advise management in collective bargaining sessions and participate in contract negotiations with the union. They also handle labor relations matters that happen every day. Arvid Anderson, director of New York City's Office of Collective Bargaining, is the country's outstanding labor "referee." He studied labor economics at the University of Wisconsin in the 1940s and says that his success "flows from an insistence on being low-keyed, methodical, and totally committed to the concept of collective bargaining."

What Education and Skills Will I Need?

High School: Preparation for college, with emphasis on English and social studies.

College: Personnel and labor relations people come from a great variety of college majors. Some have been in business administration, psychology, sociology, or industrial relations. Most companies look for a college graduate with the personal characteristics they think would be good for the company. A law degree is becoming highly desirable for contract negotiations in labor relations.

Computer skills: Skill level 3—READ, ENTER, PRINT. Personnel departments keep their data on computer information systems. They must be able to call up the information, enter new data, and print it out.

Personal skills: Ability to speak and write effectively, work as a member of a team, see opposing viewpoints, and work with people of all different levels of education are necessary skills in personnel and labor relations.

How Many Personnel and Labor Relations Workers Are There and Where Do They Work?

There are 203,000 personnel and labor relations workers, of which half are women (mostly in personnel) and 9 percent are black. Most (19 percent) work for manufacturers, others for business associations (12 percent), federal government (12 percent), and labor unions (11 percent). There are many more women than men in personnel; the reverse is true in labor relations, and the highest paying jobs are filled by men.

How Much Money Will I Make

The federal government started personnel workers at $13,800 with a bachelor's degree, and at $21,000 with a master's degree in 1985. The average salary for personnel in 1984 was $25,000. Directors of personnel made from $35,444 to $65,874. Labor relations workers earned more than those in personnel; their average was $37,500 in 1984.

What Are the Job Opportunities?

Opportunities in personnel jobs for the new graduate are very limited and competitive. Labor relations jobs are even more difficult. The best chances will be for those with a master's degree in industrial relations and for those with a law degree.

Related Careers

Employment counselor   Psychologist
Career counselor

Where Can I Get More Information?

American Society for Personnel Administration
606 North Washington Street
Alexandria, Virginia 22314

National Labor Relations Board
1717 Pennsylvania Avenue, NW
Washington, D.C. 20570

PURCHASING AGENT

Negotiates and contracts to purchase equipment, supplies, and other merchandise for a firm

What's It Like To Be a Purchasing Agent?

Purchasing agents, sometimes called industrial buyers, are responsible for getting the best dollar value for supplies for their firms. They buy raw materials, office supplies, furniture, and business machines. A purchasing agent checks on deliveries to be sure the work flow of the firm isn't interrupted because of lack of materials. He or she works with other departments within the company, such as engineering and shipping, in order to coordinate the supplies with those who need them. Nonprofit organizations such as schools, hospitals, libraries, and museums are increasingly hiring purchasing managers who figure out how to fund purchases as well as how to find the most cost-effective buys. Read "Assistant to the President," Gail Harrity Tilney's career development story on page 32, for a fascinating example of a purchasing agent's job.

What Education and Skills Will I Need?

High school: Preparation for college. Large firms hire college graduates for their training programs.

College: Many agents come from backgrounds in engineering, accounting, and economics. The top jobs go to MBA graduates.

Computer skills: Skill level 3—READ, ENTER, PRINT. Most agents keep their inventory, purchasing needs, and prices on computers. They must be able to call up the information, enter new data, and print out.

Personal skills: Skill in analyzing numbers and technical data; making buying decisions and spending within a budget; the ability to work and get along with others; and memory for detail are all necessary skills for a purchasing agent.

How Many Purchasing Agents Are There and Where Do They Work?

There are 191,000 purchasing agents; 36 percent are women and 5 percent are black. The federal government employs 14 percent of them, another 22 percent work for nondurable goods and machinery manufacturers, 7 percent are in business services, 7 percent in transportation equipment manufacturing, and still another 7 percent in electronic manufacturing.

How Much Money Will I Make?

In 1984, purchasing agents started at an average of $20,200 a year. Experienced agents earned from $24,700 to $30,600, with the top 10 percent making more than $39,000.

What Are the Job Opportunities?

Graduates who have a master's in business administration (MBA) and a bachelor's degree in purchasing, engineering, science, or business will have the best opportunities. Many opportunities will arise as service-producing organizations such as hospitals, health agencies, and schools also recognize the importance of professional purchasers in reducing costs.

Related Careers

Retail buyer   Service manager
Traffic manager

Where Can I Find More Information?

National Association of Purchasing Management
PO Box 418
Oradell, New Jersey 07649

UNDERWRITER

Appraises and selects the risks an insurance company will insure

What's It Like To Be an Underwriter?

An underwriter analyzes information in insurance applications, reports from loss control consultants, medical reports, and actuarial studies that describe the probability of insured loss, and then decides whether to issue a policy. If an underwriter is too conservative in taking risks, customers will go to another company, and if an underwriter is too liberal, the company will lose profits. Ian McGregor, an underwriter in Hartford, Connecticut, specializes in property and liability insurance. His career options included a specialty in life, property, health, or commercial insurance. Many of his cases involve drivers who have had several accidents and present a high risk for poor driving. McGregor corresponds with policy holders, agents, and managers about policy risks.

What Education and Skills Will I Need?

High school: Preparation for business or liberal arts college.
College: Trainees are recruited from all kinds of college majors. Many major in mathematics or business administration, but it is not necessary. An underwriter must pass a series of examinations and advanced courses are necessary to qualify as a "fellow" of the Academy of Life Insurance Underwriters.
Personal skills: Imagination, assertiveness, ability to make quick decisions and communicate effectively are necessary for an underwriter, as well as the ability to work with detail and evaluate information.
Computer skills: Skill level 6—READ, ENTER, PRINT, SELECT, GRAPHICS, PROGRAM. Underwriters need computer literacy to analyze data and statistics. Graphics are necessary to simplify and communicate the complex statistics of their job.

How Many Underwriters Are There and Where Do they Work?

There are 76,000 underwriters, with very few women or blacks. Almost half work for fire, marine, and casualty insurance companies, 39 percent work for insurance agents and brokers, and fourteen percent are in life insurance. They work in the insurance centers of the country in New York, San Francisco, Chicago, Dallas, Philadelphia, and Hartford.

How Much Money Will I Make?

The median salary was $21,500 a year in 1984. Experienced underwriters made about $27,000 a year, supervisors made $31,000 a year, and managers averaged $37,000. Most insurance companies have liberal vacation policies and better-than-average benefits.

What Are the Job Opportunities?

Jobs are expected to be good through the 1980s as changes in regulations and laws increase the need for underwriters. A growing number of consumer lawsuits, demand for insurance coverage for working women, and growing security consciousness all add to the demand for more insurance protection and jobs.

Related Careers

Auditor
Credit manager

Loan officer
Real estate appraiser

Where Can I Get More Information?

Insurance Information Institute
110 William Street
New York, New York 20006

American Council of Life Insurance
1850 K Street, NW
Washington, D.C. 20006

BUSINESS: ADVERTISING AND MARKETING

ABOUT THESE CAREERS

Outside of television and movies, advertising, marketing, and public relations are the most competitive, glamorous, and popular careers in New York City and many other major cities in the country. Finding ways to sell products and services to the consumer is big business. So big, in fact, that businesses pay $300 per American citizen per year for public exposure in the form of handbills, posters, newspaper ads, TV commercials, radio spots, billboards, and direct mail.

There are about 286,000 jobs in advertising, marketing, and public relations. Many employers prefer college graduates who have a liberal arts education with degrees in journalism or business. However, there is no correlation between a particular educational background and success in these fields. Hustle, enthusiasm, creativity, and aggressiveness are the requisites for success, not college degrees.

People in advertising work under great pressure. They are expected to produce quality ads in as short a time as possible. Sometimes, they must work long and irregular hours in order to make last-minute changes in ads and meet deadlines. Advertising can be a satisfying career for men and women who enjoy variety, excitement, creative challenges, and competition. Unlike people in many other careers, advertising workers experience the satisfaction of having their work in print, on television, or on radio, even though they themselves remain unknown to the public.

The marketing field is loaded with MBA graduates who find fascinating careers in advertising and selling America's products and services. They start as assistant brand managers and work up to product managers, looking for new avenues of potential sales. Advancement is very competitive in advertising, public relations, and marketing. Professionals are highly qualified in this industry and by necessity it attracts the aggressive workers.

The most successful workers of major advertising, public relations, or marketing firms advance by becoming officers and partners of the firms or they leave to establish their own agencies.

ADVERTISING

**Persuades people to buy a firm's products
or use a firm's services**

What's It Like To Be in Advertising?

To many people, Madison Avenue in New York City represents the pinnacle of glamour and success in an advertising career. But wherever the company is located, the job is a creative and challenging one and the salary can be very high. The commodity is the person's talent and the person must produce the idea, the copy, and the business that will make the client's product profitable. Careers in advertising include a number of different positions: *advertising managers,* who are responsible for planning budgets and for overall supervision; *creative workers* such as *writers, artists,* and *designers,* who develop and produce print and radio and television commercials; and *business* and *sales workers,* who handle the arrangements for broadcasting commercials on radio and TV, for publishing ads in newspapers or magazines, or for mailing them directly to the public.

Lyn Salzberg, one of the few women in a top management advertising job, is a senior vice president at Dancer, Fitzgerald Sample, a major New York advertising agency. In addition to handling accounts, Salzberg has developed one of the outstanding training programs for new recruits just beginning their advertising careers. She loves the challenge of being a woman who has "made it," and she thinks it's worth the constant planning, attention to detail, and long hours it took to get there.

What Education and Skills Will I Need?

High school: College preparatory program, with as much work in language as possible. Writing skills are particularly important. Working on school publications, learning to be a good observer, noticing how people respond, and selling are experiences that will be helpful in advertising.

College: Most advertising agencies prefer a liberal arts graduate with a major in advertising, marketing, journalism, or business. Community college, business college, and art programs can get you started in advertising. The most common way to enter the field of advertising without a degree is to begin in a department store advertising program.

Personal skills: Imagination, creativity, and a flair for language and selling are required for success in advertising.

Computer skills: Skill level 5—READ, ENTER, PRINT, SELECT, GRAPHICS. Many advertising personnel need to use graphics for copy and design. A career in management will require level 3, and account executives will keep their records on computers and also need level 3.

How Many Advertising Workers Are There and Where Do They Work?

Almost half of the 170,000 people in advertising work in New York and Chicago. About 100,000 of them work in advertising agencies. The rest work for manufacturers, retail stores, broadcasting stations, and publishers.

How Much Money Will I Make?

The top beginning salaries are paid to outstanding liberal arts graduates, usually men. In 1984, they started at $16,000 to $21,000 a year. Those with an MBA often started at $25,000 a year. Salaries vary according to the size of the agency. An account executive in a large New York agency often makes from $40,000 to $75,000 a year, and a few make much more.

Related Careers

Public relations
Fund-raiser

Lobbyist
Promotion manager

Where Can I Get More Information?

American Advertising Federation
1225 Connecticut Avenue, NW
Washington, D.C. 20036

American Association of Advertising Agencies
666 Third Avenue
New York, New York 10017

MARKETING

**Evaluates the product, the consumer, and
the marketplace and defines new avenues of
potential business growth for products and
services**

What's It Like To Be in Marketing?

Pressured! Marketing people have a simple criterion to measure their success—or failure. Sales. Everything they do either produces more sales or it doesn't. They use market research to plan, implement, and analyze surveys to learn more about the consumers' wants, needs, and spending patterns. This information provides the direction for the sales component of the company, as well as its advertising and public relations programs. Marketing information is used to determine brand names, packaging, product design, and new outlets for the company, among other management decisions. Manufacturers plan their product strategy, positioning, and promotional and pricing strategies through their market research information. Marketing is a fascinating and challenging job, one that is attracting top MBA students because of its influence on company business strategies. Marketing is one of the best places to learn a business. Top management often comes out of marketing.

What Education and Skills Will I Need?

High school: Preparation for college, with emphasis on English and mathematics.
College: Attend business, community, or four-year college. Many marketing people are coming from the nation's top MBA programs.
Computer skills: Skill level 5—READ, ENTER, PRINT, SELECT, GRAPHICS. Graphics are necessary for creative work and for research reports.
Personal skills: Decision-making skills, assertiveness, and an interest in business and profits are important.

How Many Marketing Workers Are There and Where Do They Work?

There are about 77,000 marketing people, and most of them work in New York and Chicago. About 80 percent work for companies, and the remainder work for marketing consulting firms.

How Much Money Will I Make?

In 1984, marketing professionals earned from $21,000 to $40,700. The median salary was $25,800 for all marketing workers. The top 10 percent made more than $52,000.

What Are the Job Opportunities?

Marketing is a growing field, but the numbers of highly qualified students attracted to it are growing faster. Very competitive for the beginning jobs, and for promotions. The growth in health-care facilities will result in good job opportunities for marketing for nonprofit institutions and organizations, a new career area.

Related Careers

Business manager   Advertising
Public relations

Where Can I Get More Information?

American Marketing Association
250 Wacker Street
Chicago, Illinois 60606

PUBLIC RELATIONS

**Develops and distributes persuasive
materials in order to create a favorable
public reputation**

What's It Like To Be in Public Relations?

Public relations (PR) people plan publicity that they think will be most effective, communicate with the people who would use the publicity, write press releases for newspapers and magazines, and write brochures and pamphlets about a company or product. They arrange special speaking engagements for company officials and often write speeches. They work with films, slides, video, and all types of audiovisual equipment. They often work under tension and pressure caused by tight deadlines and last-minute changes in schedules. Public relations workers must be knowledgeable about all media and decide what the most effective way is to put across their ideas. Michael Wolf, a Cincinnati PR man just starting his own firm, has had four years of experience in Chicago. He says he now works twice as hard and at much more risk, but he thinks he is where he wants to be—using every idea he ever had. "My long hours seem to be easier on the family, now that the business is my own. Besides that, they wanted to be back in Cincinnati, the place they consider home."

What Education and Skills Will I Need?

High school: Preparation for junior college or four-year college.
College: Major in English, journalism, or a field that interests

you and in which you want to do public relations work. Public relations people come from a wide variety of college majors, including liberal arts and the applied arts. Writing skills are mandatory.

Computer skills: Skill level 5—READ, ENTER, PRINT, SELECT, GRAPHICS. Graphics are necessary for creative work and for research reports.

Personal skills: Self-confidence, assertiveness, an outgoing personality, understanding of human behavior, enthusiasm, and imagination are important for success in public relations.

How Many Public Relations Workers Are There and Where Do They Work?

There are 95,000 public relations workers and half of them are women; 3 percent are black; 12 percent work part time. Most PR people are working in New York, Los Angeles, Chicago, and Washington.

How Much Money Will I Make?

In 1984, the median income for all PR workers was $25,800 a year, the range from $21,000 to $40,700. The median salary for top-level public relations people was $44,000 with the top ten percent making over $52,000 a year.

What Are the Job Opportunities?

Public relations jobs are very competitive because thousands of college graduates who want to work in cities look for a job with glamour, like public relations. Chances will be best for enthusiastic people with sound academic credentials and some media experience.

Related Careers

Advertising	Fund-raiser and developer
Lobbyist	Marketing

Where Can I Get More Information?

Public Relations Society of America, Inc.
845 Third Avenue
New York, New York 10022

BUSINESS: COMPUTER OPERATIONS

ABOUT THESE CAREERS

By 1995 there will be 350,000 programmers and systems analysts; these are among the top 20 fastest growing careers.

Most college graduates will be in the following computer jobs: systems analysis and programming, sales, software development, computer consulting, operations, and management.

Most of the growth in the computer industry will result from advances in computer capabilities. There are three major areas of new technologies: hardware—the machinery that is getting smaller, cheaper, and faster; software—the programs or instructions that tell the hardware what to do, and the language the instructions are written in; and applications—the kinds of work computers can perform. Employment is clustered around major cities. The education and training of computer personnel will continue to be inadequate for the demand.

The following list of professional computer job descriptions gives you an idea of what the college-level computer jobs are.

Computer Operations Careers

1. *Corporate Director of Data Processing:* Directs computer processing; the top executive for all computer processing.
2. *Technical Assistant:* Works as a member of corporate director's staff; usually head of advanced planning for data processing (DP) function.
3. *Services Coordinator/User Liaison:* Coordinates DP activities with other functions or departments.
4. *Manager of Systems Analysis:* Analyzes how DP can be applied to user problems; designs effective and efficient DP solutions.

5. *Lead Systems Analyst:* Helps plan, organize, and control the activities of the systems analysis section.
6. *Senior Systems Analyst:* Confers with users to define DP projects, formulates problems, and designs solutions.
7. *Systems Analyst:* Works with users to define DP projects or project segments, or irons out details in specifications.
8. *Systems Analyst Trainee:* Usually has some DP experience; expected to spend time learning rather than producing.
9. *Manager of Applications Programming:* Responsible for the development of effective, efficient, well-documented programs.
10. *Lead Applications Programmer:* Helps plan, organize, and control section activities.
11. *Senior Systems Programmer:* Specializes in support, maintenance, and use of one or more operating systems; able to work at highest levels of programming.
12. *Applications Programmer:* Works on only one or a few applications.
13. *Applications Progammer Trainee:* Learns to program under supervision.
14. *Programming Team Librarian:* Keeps track of program revisions.
15. *Manager of Systems Programming:* Plans and directs the activities of the programming section; assigns personnel to projects.
16. *Lead Systems Programmer:* Helps plan, organize, and control the activities of the programming section.
17. *Senior Systems Programmer:* Specializes in support, maintenance, and use of one or more operating systems; able to work at highest levels of programming.
18. *Systems Programmer:* Specializes in the support of one or a few operating system components or subsystems.
19. *Systems Programming Trainee:* Has a good background in DP and knows or is learning assembler language.
20. *Program Librarian:* Maintains the on-line and off-line libraries of production programs in source and object form.
21. *Manager of Data Base Administration:* Plans, organizes, and schedules activities of the data base administration section.
22. *Data Base Administrator:* Analyzes company's computerized information requirements; coordinates data collection with storage needs; organizes data.
23. *Data Communications Telecommunications Manager:* Designs data communications networks and is responsible for installation and operation of data links.

24. *Data Communications Analyst:* Specializes in network design, traffic analysis, and data communications software.

COMPUTER PROGRAMMER

**Writes detailed instructions called
programs that list in logical order the steps
the computer must follow to solve a
problem**

What's It Like To Be a Computer Programmer?

There are two kinds of computer programmers: systems programmer and applications programmer. A systems programmer, sometimes called a software systems engineer, gives a particular computer the ability to perform detailed tasks. For example, a systems programmer determines the specific computer language that will be used and which functions should get priority. An applications programmer uses the language and tasks already established by the systems programmer to write programs that tell the computer exactly what to do. "An applications programmer can work quite independently and at his or her own pace, and can progress pretty much as fast as he or she is capable," says Doris Schwartz, a recent college graduate who is a full-time computer programmer with IBM. "Most days we spend an entire day writing a program for the computers, or correcting errors in a program that's already written. If we are in the process of designing a program system—preparing a series of programs, for example, to keep track of production and take inventory—we may spend several hours discussing methods and details with our customers. We often run the computers ourselves, testing progress. Attending classes and lectures is important since the field is changing and growing so fast."

What Education and Skills Will I Need?

High school: Preparation for college, with as many mathematics and computer courses as possible.

College: Programmers are hired from business colleges, two-year community colleges, and four-year colleges. Most programmers are college graduates. Major in mathematics, computer science, business, or whatever field you want to work in, such as health or engineering.

Computer skills: Skill level 6—READ, ENTER, PRINT, SELECT, GRAPHICS, PROGRAM. Programmers need the optimum level of skills.

Personal skills: The work calls for patience, persistence, and the ability to be extremely accurate. Imagination and logical thinking are important for programmers who work out new solutions to problems.

How Many Computer Programmers Are There and Where Do They Work?

There are 341,000 computer programmers; 32 percent are women, 5.7 percent are black, and 5.4 percent work part time. Most programmers are employed by data processing service organizations—including firms that write and sell software (18 percent), finance, insurance, and real estate firms (15 percent), and office, computing, and accounting machine manufacturing firms (9 percent).

How Much Money Will I Make?

In 1984, the average beginning salary in private industry was $385 a week. Experienced programmers received $475 a week. The median salary for all programmers was $500 a week. The top 10 percent made over $780 a week.

What Are the Job Opportunities?

Computer programmers are expected to be fourth in the top 20 fastest-growing occupations, projected to 1995. The increase will be in high-level jobs. The systems and applications programmers with the best education for complex work will be most in demand.

Related Careers

Systems analyst   Mathematician
Statistician   Engineer

Where Can I Get More Information?

American Federation of Information Processing Societies
210 Summit Avenue
Montvale, New Jersey 07645

Data Processing Management Association
505 Busse Highway
Park Ridge, Illinois, 60068

SYSTEMS ANALYST

**Decides how data are collected, prepared
for the computers, processed, stored, and
made available to users**

What's It Like To Be a Systems Analyst?

Sally Aarons, a mathematics major at Stanford was accepted in a major computer training program. After some work experience in programming, she is back in training as a systems analyst. Systems analysts are the problem solvers for the computer user. The systems analyst begins work by discussing with managers the jobs to be performed. She learns exactly what kind of information is needed, what has to be done with it, how quickly it has to be processed, and how it is currently being collected and recorded. In most companies, the analyst evaluates the computer equipment already owned by the company in order to determine if it can carry the additional data or if new equipment is needed. Next, the analyst develops the computer system—that is, decides how the data should be prepared for the machines, processed, stored, and made available to users. If the company decides to adopt the proposed system, the analyst prepares specifications for computer programmers to follow. Analysts usually specialize in business, scientific, or engineering applications. The problems systems analysts deal with range from monitoring nuclear fission in a power plant to forecasting sales for a publisher.

Robert D. McCaffrey, married and father of a six-year-old, is a systems analyst supervisor at General Electric. His day starts with a review of the previous night's computer processing to make sure that all regularly scheduled programs have run normally. Next, he reviews the progress being made on new development programs and systems to ensure that schedules are being met or remedial action is being taken. Daily meetings with people who are using the data are held to discuss new development and maintenance projects. Usually, a weekly meeting is held with all programmers to review the previous week's activity and modify short-term plans if necessary. Also, meetings with management are held to review long-term plans to ensure the proper resource application.

What Education and Skills Will I Need?

High school: Preparation for college, with as much mathematics as possible.

College: Systems analysts come from majors in engineering, computer science, accounting, mathematics, and economics. Regardless of the major, they must know programming languages. Most systems analysts come from other careers and learn the necessary skills in adult and corporate education courses.

Computer skills: Skill level 6—READ, ENTER, PRINT, SELECT, GRAPHICS, PROGRAM. Analysts need maximum computer proficiency.

Personal skills: The ability to concentrate and pay close attention to detail is important. Must be able to communicate well with technical personnel, such as programmers and managers, as well as with people who have no computer background.

How Many Systems Analysts Are There and Where Do They Work?

There are 245,000 systems analysts; 26 percent are women, 5.8 percent are black, and 2.5 percent work part time. Most analysts enter this job from other jobs such as engineer, manager, or computer programmer. More than half of the jobs are in urban areas with manufacturing firms (20 percent), computer and data processing services (17 percent), finance, insurance, and real estate businesses (12 percent), and government (11 percent).

How Much Money Will I Make?

In 1984, the median salary for analysts was $600 a week. The top 10 percent made over $870 a week.

What Are the Job Opportunities?

Employment is expected to rise as advances in technology increase computer capabilities leading to new applications for computers. Computer systems analysts are third in the top 20 fastest growing occupations. The number of people employed in this field is expected to reach 350,000 by 1995. New applications will be found in factory and office automation, telecommunications, and scientific research. College graduates in computer science with a few years' experience in the work world will get the jobs.

Related Careers

Computer programmer   Engineer
Mathematician   Actuary

Where Can I Get More Information?

Association for Systems Management
24587 Bagley Road
Cleveland, Ohio 44138

American Federation of Information Processing Societies
1815 North Lynn Street
Arlington, Virginia 22209

BUSINESS: MONEY MANAGEMENT

ABOUT THESE CAREERS

There are over 1.5 million jobs in these four money-management careers—accountant, actuary, bank officer, credit manager. Most of the jobs are held by men.

Money management requires a college education, and for banking, a well-organized office training program ranging from six months to one year is the best preparation.

Advancement in money management depends largely on job performance and the qualifying examinations in accounting and actuarial work, which require specialized study. Courses in every phase of banking are offered by the American Institute of Banking, an industry-sponsored school.

Money managers work in attractive, comfortable offices. Since a great deal of bank business and credit business depends on customers' impressions, money managers are encouraged to wear conservative, somewhat formal business clothes. Most jobs require no travel, although accountants employed by national accounting firms may travel extensively to conduct audits and perform other services for their clients. Most money managers work overtime, and some are constantly studying at home for the qualifying examinations necessary for advancement. The first 10 years in a money-management career limits the time for social and family life outside of work.

ACCOUNTANT

**Designs and controls financial records and
verifies financial data**

What's It Like To Be an Accountant?

Accountants prepare financial reports, profit and loss studies, cost studies, and tax reports. The three major accounting fields are public, management, and government accounting. Public accountants are independent and work on a fee basis for businesses, individuals, or accounting firms. Management accountants, also called industrial or private accountants, handle the financial resources of their company and work on a salary basis. Government accountants examine financial resources of government agencies and audit private businesses to see whether government regulations are being observed. Any of these accountants may specialize in auditing, taxes, cost accounting, budgeting and control, or investments. Sue Jourdon, Certified Public Accountant (CPA) for a small city, likes her work because she has the challenge of revising the city's present accounting system so it can be put onto a computer. She has a liberal arts college background with summer work experience in computer programming. "The hours are too long during the tax season— 10 to 12 hours a day. But the good pay makes up for it." Marcel Renaud, CPA, says an accountant must love figures, and the study never stops. "It's a science and you must keep up to date, reading three to five hours a week." Renaud has specialized in health care, and at 32, is making well over $75,000 figuring out innovative ways to bill rocketing health-care costs to government and insurance plans that will pay.

What Education and Skills Will I Need?

High school: A college preparatory program and strong interest and ability in mathematics is necessary for a certified public accountant program. Alternatives include a commercial course leading to a business college program or community college program in accounting, correspondence study in accounting, or a college course leading to a business administration major.
College: Accounting is offered as a one-year business college

program, a two-year community college program, and a four-year college program. Nine out of ten CPAs are college graduates, have passed the CPA examination in the state in which they work, and have had two years of accounting experience before taking the exam. In the near future, some states may require CPA candidates to have a graduate degree. Increasingly, computer programming skills are required.

Computer skills: Skill level 5—READ, ENTER, PRINT, SELECT, GRAPHICS. Accountants do much of their spread sheets on a computer, and use graphics to illustrate the company's financial data.

Personal skills: Aptitude for mathematics and for working with systems and computers; ability to work independently; accuracy; and a high standard of integrity are necessary in an accounting career.

How Many Accountants Are There and Where Do They Work?

There are 856,000 accountants; 39 percent are women, 5 percent are black and 6 percent are employed part time. The majority work in urban centers for accounting firms (20 percent), manufacturing (17 percent), and government (13 percent).

How Much Money Will I Make?

In 1984, starting salaries for accountants averaged $19,500 a year. Beginners with master's degrees started at $23,200 a year. Accountants with experience averaged from $30,000 to $47,400 a year. Chief accountants earned $70,000 and more.

Related Careers

Appraiser	Actuary
Budget officer	Bank officer

Where Can I Get More Information?

National Association of Accountants
PO Box 433
Montvale, New Jersey 07645

National Society of Public Accountants
1010 North Fairfax Street
Alexandria, Virginia, 22314

ACTUARY

**Assembles and analyzes statistics in order
to design profitable insurance and
pension plans**

What's It Like To Be an Actuary?

Why do teenage boys pay more for car insurance? How much is a life insurance policy for a 21-year-old female? Answers to these and similar questions are provided by actuaries. They calculate probabilities of death, sickness, injury, disability, unemployment, retirement, and property loss from accidents, theft, and fire. They use statistics to construct probability tables in order to develop insurance rates. They usually work for a life insurance or liability insurance company. Actuary Mark Magnus, of New England Life Insurance Company in Boston, specializes in pension plans. This involves making sure that employers invest enough money wisely for retired workers to get a monthly pension for life. Magnus cautions college graduates to plan on a limited social life for the first few years as an actuary because the required actuarial examinations take 15 to 25 hours a week of home study. Or, he recommends, date another actuary and study together!

What Education and Skills Will I Need?

High school: College preparatory course, with as much mathematics as possible.

College: A degree is required, with a good background in calculus, probability and statistics, and computer science. While still in college, you should begin to take the examinations required to become a professional actuary; it takes from 5 to 10 years to complete the exams after college while on the job. There are 34 colleges that offer a degree in actuarial science. Employers generally prefer applicants with a degree in actuarial science, and those who have passed several examinations offered by professional actuarial societies.

Computer skills: Skill level 5—READ, PRINT, ENTER, SELECT, GRAPHICS. Actuaries work with computers, using graphics routinely.

Personal skills: Mathematical skills, interest in studying and working independently to pass examinations, and ability to do routine detailed work are needed.

How Many Actuaries Are There and Where Do They Work?

There are 10,000 professional actuaries in the United States and most of them are men. Almost half are employed in the five cities with major life insurance companies: New York, Hartford, Chicago, Philadelphia, and Boston. Others work for engineering and architectural firms (23 percent), for insurance agents and brokers (14 percent), and for fire, marine, and casualty insurance companies (13 percent).

How Much Money Will I Make?

In 1984, starting salaries for college graduates who had not yet passed any actuarial exams were from $18,000 to $21,000 a year. The pay increases rapidly as the exams are passed. Beginners who have passed one exam started at $21,000 to $23,000; those who have passed two exams started at $22,000 to $25,000 a year. Associates made from $30,000 to $35,000; and fellows earned from $40,000 to $50,000.

What Are the Job Opportunities?

Opportunities are expected to be very good through the 1980s. Because of the rising numbers of insurance policies of all kinds, and the expanding group health and life insurance plans, employment in the actuarial field will increase as the health occupations increase. The best jobs and the most money will go to the graduates who have passed two or more actuary examinations while they are still in college.

Related Careers

Mathematician   Financial analyst
Statistician   Engineering analyst
Economist

Where Can I Get More Information?

American Society of Pension Actuaries
1413 K Street, NW, 5th floor
Washington, D.C. 20005

Society of Actuaries
500 Park Boulevard, Room 440
Itasca, Illinois 60143

BANK OFFICER

**Banks are in the "money" business and
bank officers are responsible for the
management of the bank's
business**

What's It Like To Be a Bank Officer?

"If you're interested in money management," says Ian Burnham,
"a bank training program is a good place to learn." Officers in
a bank include the loan officer, who makes decisions on loan
applications within the policies of the bank; trust officer, who
manages property, funds, or real estate for clients, including
financial planning, investment, and taxes; operations officer,
who oversees the efficiency of bank procedures; customer manager, who is responsible for relations with customers and other
banks; branch manager, who has full responsibility for a branch
office; personnel administrator; and public relations and oper-
ational research officers.

As banking rules and regulations change, and as banks take
on new investment activities, the job provides new creative opportunities. Investment markets change rapidly, creating a need
for bright, flexible, innovative investment bankers who will earn
excellent salaries.

What Education and Skills Will I Need?

High school: Preparation for college, with emphasis on mathematics and economics.

College: Bank management trainees usually must have a bachelor's degree in business administration with a major in finance, or a liberal arts degree with a major in accounting, economics, commercial law, or statistics. Some banks prefer trainees who have a master's degree in business administration (MBA). Small city and rural banks promote outstanding clerks and tellers to management positions.

Computer skills: Skill level 5—READ, ENTER, PRINT, SELECT, GRAPHICS. All finance managers must have graphics computer skills as a tool in their routine work.

Personal skills: Ability to analyze detailed information, interest in working independently, good judgment in advising others, and tact are needed in banking. Investment banking requires high motivation and risk taking—the same skills stockbrokers must have.

How Many Bank Officers Are There and Where Do They Work?

There are 424,000 bank officers and managers; 37 percent are women, 3 percent are black, and 2 percent work part time. They work in every bank in the country—from rural banks to big city banks with well-developed training programs for managers.

How Much Money Will I Make?

In 1984, beginning college graduates in officer training programs of large banks started at $13,200 to $22,000 a year. Those with master's degrees started with slightly more, and those with MBAs started from $21,600 to $42,000 their first year! Bank officers averaged $28,600, and the top 10 percent made over $52,000. The officers of small-town banks work up from tellers and are paid much less than city bankers.

Master of business administration graduates with little or no experience are starting at $50,000 a year in investment banking. With an undergraduate degree, they start at $30,000 if other qualifications are outstanding. Liberal arts graduates start at lower salaries but they show high growth potential as they end up in top management jobs.

What Are the Job Opportunities?

Chances for work as a bank officer will be competitive through the 1980s. More services and a greater use of computers will require sound management and more jobs, but the number of applicants has increased. Promotions from junior to senior officers will be as competitive as they have always been.

Related Careers

Purchasing agent   Stockbroker
Business manager   Industrial relations director

Where Can I Get More Information?

American Bankers Association
1120 Connecticut Avenue, NW
Washington, D.C. 20036

CREDIT MANAGER

**Decides which individuals or businesses are
eligible for credit, according to a company's
credit policy**

What's It Like To Be a Credit Manager?

Coins and paper money are on the way out. Computerized credit is on its way in. Soon, credit managers will be dealing with how to identify creditworthy individuals through a special watch that monitors their blood pressure and pulse. In the meantime, credit managers decide who can receive credit by analyzing detailed financial reports of businesses (commercial credit) or bank records, credit bureau recommendations, and applications of individuals (consumer credit). They are also responsible for establishing the company's credit policy and setting financial standards on the basis of the amount of risk the company can take. They often work with salespeople in developing the company's credit policy.

What Education and Skills Will I Need?

High school: Preparation for a two-year or a four-year college.
College: Most credit managers have a college degree in business administration, accounting, or economics in order to get into the good training programs. Others have finished a two-year accounting or business administration program. Computer skills are crucial for all career levels in credit.
Computer skills: Skill level 6—READ, ENTER, PRINT, SELECT, GRAPHICS, PROGRAM. Computer literacy is essential for credit managers.
Personal skills: Ability to analyze details and draw logical conclusions, a pleasant personality, and speaking skills are necessary for success as a credit manager.

How Many Credit Managers Are There and Where Do They Work?

Of the 55,000 credit managers, 60 percent are men. Most work in urban areas. About half work for wholesale and retail trade, and one-third work for manufacturers and banks.

How Much Money Will I Make?

In 1984, trainees with college degrees started at $13,000 to $21,000 a year. Experienced credit managers averaged from $22,000 to 28,000 a year. The top-level jobs paid over $52,000 a year.

What Are the Job Opportunities?

Jobs are going to be competitive in credit management through the 1980s. Credit has increased very rapidly and is here to stay. As firms strive to get the biggest sales of their products and services, there will be a greater demand for skilled credit managers who can establish credit policies strict enough to minimize bad debt losses. Use of computers, telecommunication networks, and centralized credit will limit the growth of jobs.

Related Careers

Bank loan officer
Credit union manager
Controller

Financial institution
manager

Where Can I Get More Information?

National Association of Credit Management
475 Park Avenue South
New York, New York 10016

BUSINESS: SALES

ABOUT THESE CAREERS

Sales is where the money is. You can make the most amount of money with the least amount of education in this career group. Sales is also where the experience is, and the road to top management is often through sales. There are about 7 million salespeople in our country and 16 percent of them have college degrees. Most salespeople come from a great variety of college backgrounds, although manufacturers' salespeople often have technical or scientific backgrounds.

Beginning salespeople work evenings, weekends, and holidays—whenever the customers and clients are free to buy. Some manufacturers' salespeople have large territories and travel a lot. Others work in the neighborhood of their headquarters. The amount of time beginning salespeople put into building up their accounts is hard on family and friends. But once these accounts are established, a process which can take about ten years or so in areas such as stockbrokering and car sales, salespeople can meet their clients at their mutual convenience—on the golf course, on the racquetball court, or at lunch.

If you are interested in sales and have decided not to go for the big money, then you can put in fewer hours. In many fields, salespeople are free to set up their own time schedule. Real estate is the best example of flexible time. More than 25 percent of the 7 million people in sales work part time. A flexible schedule provides many opportunities for coordinating a career with parenting.

Salespeople who have managerial ability may advance to assistant sales manager, sales manager, or general manager. Some managers open their own businesses or become partners in dealerships, agencies, or firms. Most sales advancement is in terms of making more money and having more free time as customer accounts become well established.

AUTOMOBILE SALESPERSON

Sells new and used cars for car dealers

What's It Like To Be an Automobile Salesperson?

An automobile salesperson must know about *selling*, not about the complicated details of the product. The main thing is to know how to close a deal, that is, overcome the customer's hesitancy to buy. Often, a new salesperson begins a sale and an experienced one helps close the sale. A new salesperson may quote prices and must learn how to assess a trade-in allowance for the customer's present car. Salespeople often arrange financing and insurance for the cars they sell. They also have to learn to develop and follow leads to prospective customers. Car salespeople can earn anywhere from $300 to $500 on each car they sell.

Commission selling, or getting paid a percentage of the price of the product sold, is a nontraditional job for women. The higher the price of the product, the fewer women are selling it. For instance, very few women sell cars, commercial real estate, or securities—the top-paying sales jobs. An exception is Elaine Atkins, daughter of a Ford dealer, who does sell strictly on commission. She says she would never have thought of getting into car sales if it hadn't been a family business. Now that she has gone through the steps from working on salary with commissions from "walk-ins" to building her own prospects list and working strictly on commission, she loves it. She loves being her own boss, taking off a month when she has filled her quota, and making more money than she ever thought possible.

What Education and Skills Will I Need?

High school: Most, but not all, salespeople prepare for college in a great variety of majors. Usually, they are trained on the job by sales managers and experienced salespeople.
College: Many new car dealers have some college background, but business and selling experience count more than a degree.
Computer skills: Skill level 2—READ, ENTER. Car salespeople use computers to check the inventory. They need to find what's in stock, and to enter new data.
Personal skills: Sales skills, initiative, assertiveness, enthusiasm for the product, and ambition make a successful salesworker.

How Many Automobile Salespeople Are There and Where Do They Work?

There are an estimated 157,000 automobile salespeople and 114,000 work for new car dealers. They work in every city, town, and village in the country. New car dealers employ from 1 to 50 salespeople.

How Much Money Will I Make?

In 1984, salespeople in the automobile business averaged $21,000 a year. The top 10 percent made over $70,000. Earnings vary widely depending on geography, experience, and type and size of dealership.

What Are the Job Opportunities?

Anyone who can prove herself or himself a seller can convince a dealer to hire him or her for a commission job that doesn't involve a financial risk to the dealer. If selling cars is what you want to do, you can suggest a plan to a dealer (working after hours, weekends, or after another job). Ask for a few months' trial, and if the dealer makes money, you will have a job.

Related Careers

Real estate salesperson
Insurance salesperson
Stockbroker

Manufacturer's representative

Where Can I Get More Information?

National Automobile Dealers Association
8400 Westpark Drive
McLean, Virginia 22102

RETAIL AND WHOLESALE BUYER

Purchases merchandise to resell at a profit

What's It Like To Be a Retail Buyer?

Buyers purchase for resale the best available merchandise at the lowest possible price to profit from the flow of goods from manufacturer to consumer. Wholesale buyers purchase goods directly from manufacturers or from other wholesale firms for resale to retail firms. Retail buyers purchase goods from wholesale firms or, occasionally, directly from the manufacturers. Buyers work on a very busy schedule with a lot of hustle and with all kinds of people. Retail buyer Irv Lief, a former New York City Macy's trainee, has just taken a new job in merchandising at Innes of Wichita, Kansas. He loves the fast pace of the work and doesn't think it matters whether you work for a large store or a small one. "Getting the goods to the customers at the right time for the best profit is exactly the daily challenge I like to live with. My wife is also in business," says Lief, "and we both like a fast-track lifestyle."

What Education and Skills Will I Need?

High school: Preparation for business school, art school, a merchandising program, or a liberal arts degree.
College: Take a two-year or four-year course that includes business, marketing, fashion, merchandising, and art. Prepare for

a department store training program for buyers, such as the prestigious Bloomingdale's program.

Computer skills: Skill Level 3—READ, ENTER, PRINT. Buyers keep inventory and sales records on a computer and must be able to call up the information, enter new data, and print out their working lists.

Personal skills: Buyers must be able to work fast, be good planners, and be able to communicate with salesworkers, other buyers, and sellers on a day-to-day basis.

How Many Retail and Wholesale Buyers Are There and Where Do They Work?

There are 256,000 buyers and merchandising managers. Two-thirds of them are retail buyers, working for clothing and general department stores in major cities. Sixty percent are men.

How Much Money Will I Make?

In 1984, the starting salary for most buyers was between $15,100 and $22,500 a year. The median income for buyers was $19,500. The top 10 percent of all buyers made over $38,000.

What Are the Job Opportunities?

Jobs will be competitive through the 1980s since they are glamour jobs and many college graduates go for these. Assertive, fast-working people who like to hustle are the ones who will get these jobs.

Related Careers

Comparison shopper   Merchandise manager
Sales manager   Manufacturer's repre-
                              sentative

Where Can I Get More Information?

National Mass Retailing Institute
570 Seventh Avenue
New York, New York 10018

INSURANCE SALESPERSON

Sells policies that protect individuals and
businesses against future losses and
financial pressures

What's It Like To Be an Insurance Salesperson?

There are 375,000 people in insurance sales. Other insurance jobs for college graduates include managers, security analysts, underwriters, and actuaries. As insurance companies develop their financial planning services, they are expanding the kinds of careers they provide. The front-line workers are the sales-people and brokers. An insurance agent sells for one company, usually on a commission basis; a broker sells insurance for several companies. Managers are responsible for the adminis-tration of policy, accounting, investments, and loans. Under-writers review insurance applications to evaluate the risk involved in order to determine profit for the company. Accoun-tants, bookkeepers, and lawyers are also employed by insurance companies.

John E. Wilson, Jr. is a business executive for the John Han-cock Mutual Life Insurance Company. What he likes best about his work is the interaction with people. He likes motivating, guiding, and producing an end result. Wilson thinks it is im-portant for students to realize that during a career many inter-ests or circumstances develop that bring changes they might not have planned or intended. He would like to see young people plan their education with more flexibility than most think is needed. "Our top insurance sales and management people, for example, come from a great variety of college majors and work experiences. Their skills would lead them to excel in sales in any number of other fields, as well."

Monica Ladd, insurance broker in a family business, spends the day changing and rating policies, answering clients' ques-tions about coverage, talking to special agents representing their companies, and contacting people about accident reports and new information. She finds the work very stimulating because of the constant change in policies and people's needs and because she makes very good money.

What Education and Skills Will I Need?

High school: Preparation for business, two- or four-year college. **College:** Major in business administration, personnel, insurance, or liberal arts. Insurance salespeople come from all kinds of educational backgrounds, and a degree is not necessary for good sales jobs. Most insurance salespeople come from other jobs. They tend to be older than entrants to other careers. All agents and most brokers must be licensed in the state where they plan to sell insurance. The College of Insurance in New York City trains college graduates for top-level jobs in the industry.
Computer skills: Skill level 2—READ, ENTER. Salespeople keep track of their sales and prospects on the computer.
Personal skills: Enthusiasm, self-confidence, discipline, and ability to communicate well are necessary to be successful in selling. Must be able to inspire confidence.

How Many Insurance Salespeople Are There and Where Do They Work?

There are 371,000 full-time insurance agents and brokers. There is a high turnover of agents; at the end of four years only about 15 percent are still full-time agents. High turnover and high part-time activity provide all kinds of entry-level opportunities for beginners. There are insurance agencies and brokers in every city, town, and village in the country. The headquarters of insurance companies are in: California, Connecticut, Illinois, Massachusetts, Pennsylvania, New Jersey, New York, and Texas.

How Much Money Will I Make?

Beginners start at a salary of about $1,200 a month for six months before they go on commission. After five years of building a clientele, salespeople have a median income of $35,000 a year. Top agents make $55,000 and some earn over $150,000 a year.

What Are the Job Opportunities?

The insurance business is just out of its biggest slump since it began. Certainly a time of transition, there are many opportunities for innovative, skilled college graduates interested in investments. Selling jobs have a big turnover, giving many beginners an opportunity. The overall insurance industry is changing rapidly with the expansion of financial services and development. Insurance company sales represent 9 percent of the U. S. gross national product, and more if you include hospitals. That's a lot of saleswork!

Related Careers

Real estate agent   Car sales
Manufacturer's repre-   Stockbroker
   sentative

Where Can I Get More Information?

Insurance Information Institute
110 William Street
New York, New York 10038

American Council of Life Insurance
1850 K Street, NW
Washington, D.C. 20006

MANUFACTURER'S REPRESENTATIVE

Sells all manufactured products, mainly to businesses and institutions

What's It Like To Be a Manufacturer's Representative?

A manufacturer's representative, sometimes called a sales engineer, industrial salesperson, or sales rep, spends most of his or her time visiting prospective buyers to inform them about the products they sell, analyze the buyers' needs, and take orders. Representatives visit firms in their territory. They prepare reports on sales prospects or customers' credit ratings, handle correspondence, and study literature about their products. Sales reps usually promote their products by displays at conferences or by giving demonstrations to companies on how to use their products. Stacey O'Sullivan, sales rep for Wang, sells highly technical computer equipment. She says that in addition to learning all about her product, she must also be able to help prospective buyers with technical problems, show them how to use the software more effectively, and tell them what other equipment is available for expanding their computer system. It often takes months to negotiate a sale. O'Sullivan loves the challenge of selling and the money she makes in computer systems, the fastest growing product in the world.

What Education and Skills Will I Need?

High school: Preparation for college. College graduates are preferred.

College: Many technical or specialized salesworkers are engineers, pharmacists, or chemists. Others come from business or liberal arts majors. Over half of all entrants transfer from other occupations, and more than half do not have a degree.

Computer skills: Skill level 2—READ, ENTER. Salespersons need to keep track of inventory on a computer and be able to enter new sales data.

Personal skills: Selling skills, assertiveness, pleasant appearance, interest in the product, and the ability to get along well with people are needed for all saleswork.

How Many Manufacturers' Representatives Are There and Where Do They Work?

There are 547,000 manufacturers' representatives; only 20 percent are women and 3 percent black. They are employed by the printing and publishing, chemicals, fabricated metal products, electrical, and other machinery industries, as well as the transportation and food products industries. Most work out of branch offices, usually in big cities near prospective customers.

How Much Money Will I Make?

In 1984, the median salary was $23,400 a year. The highest salaries were in electrical and electronics equipment, construction materials and pharmaceuticals. The majority of salesworkers get paid a combination of salary, commission, and bonus. The top 10 percent make more than $44,200 a year.

What Are the Job Opportunities?

Jobs will be good for well-trained and ambitious people through the 1980s.

Related Careers

Real estate salesperson   Retail buyer
Car salesperson   Stockbroker

Where Can I Get More Information?

Manufacturers' Agents National Association
PO Box 16878
Irvine, California 92713

REAL ESTATE SALESPERSON

Represents property owners who want to sell or rent residential and commercial properties

What's It Like To Be a Real Estate Salesperson?

Anne DeMarzo, number one agent for the biggest rental agency in New York City, started as a trainee stationed in one building to show apartments. She got her real estate license the following July, and that month rented 18 apartments. She makes a lot of money—$100,000 last year. Starting at her desk with telephone calls to clients, she spends a lot of time going over apartment listings and deciding which would be just right for them. She credits her success primarily to a knack for remembering hundreds of apartments listings.

More experienced Neil Gallagher, number one salesperson for another agency in New York City, says the key to top sales is to show precisely the right apartments to customers. The best job a salesperson can do, he said, "is in the selection of *what* to show, because anyone can show an apartment or house or building." He always visits what he is going to sell before he shows it, checking size of bedrooms, dramatic views, and any unique features he can use to make it special for particular clients.

What Education and Skills Will I Need?

A college degree is not required in order to be a real estate salesperson or broker, although a state real estate license is required. More than 200 colleges and many correspondence schools offer one or more courses in real estate to qualify for the real estate examination. Ability to sell is the key to success in real estate careers.

Computer skills: Skill level 2—READ, ENTER. Salespeople check their listings on the office computer, and enter new data and sales.

Personal skills: Pleasant personality and appearance, assertiveness, enthusiasm, tact, a good memory for faces, names, and listings make a successful real estate salesperson.

How Many Real Estate Salespeople Are There and Where Do They Work?

There are 363,000 full-time agents and brokers; half are women, and less than 1 percent are black. This is a career known for part-time workers; there are over 4 million licensed realtors. Most are in small firms and self-employed.

How Much Money Will I Make?

Commissions on sales are the means of income in the real estate business. Commissions vary from 5 to 10 percent, depending on the type of property and the part of the country; Vermonters make much less than agents in San Francisco or New York City. The median income is $19,000 for salesworkers, and $31,600 for brokers. Top salesman Neil Gallagher makes $300,000 in New York City.

What Are the Job Opportunities?

Good jobs in real estate are very competitive and will continue to be so. The best chances for work will go to the well-trained, ambitious people who enjoy selling. The housing market and economy always influence the job market. There is great turnover in the field; beginners are often discouraged because they can't close enough sales deals to get started.

Related Careers

Car salesperson
Stockbroker

Insurance salesperson
Manufacturer's representative

Where Can I Get More Information?

National Association of Realtors
430 North Michigan Avenue
Chicago, Illinois 60611

STOCKBROKER

Sells stocks, bonds, or mutual funds to individuals and institutions

What's It Like To Be a Stockbroker?

A stockbroker, sometimes called a securities salesperson, gets an order for stock and relays the order through the firm's order room to the floor of a securities exchange or the firm's trading department. After this transaction is completed, the stockbroker notifies the customer of the sale. Other duties of the broker include explaining the stock market and trading practices to customers, suggesting when to buy and when to sell, and often, managing the money of institutions with millions of dollars to invest. Argie Economou, associate vice-president with Dean Witter Reynolds, didn't even know what a stockbroker was after three years in premed, one year in economics, and one year in the corporate world before he served in the Vietnam War. He watched a young stockbroker who was an army second lieutenant persuade fellow officers to invest their money rather than throw it away. When he returned to the corporate world, he found he had been bitten by the bug of finance and investments. In 1970, he was offered a job in New York. His training included six months at the New York Institute of Finance and a lot of backroom paperwork and study on his first job. After 15 years in business, despite the valleys and peaks, he wouldn't be anywhere else. "I'm my own boss," explains Economou. "I can come and go as I please. I can make 126 phone calls in one day, as I have done, or I can take off and make none. It's a moving business of endless variety. Everything you see in this world—everything you see or smell or touch—relates to business. It's all-consuming and I love it."

Ann Williams, a young lawyer from Arkansas, decided to change careers when a former professor needed a sales assistant in the securities business. She had been working for the Arkansas legislature, looking for an opportunity to move to the Big Apple. On the job for the required six months before taking and passing the necessary securities examination, Williams stayed in her first job for a little less than a year. She went on to another short-term job before going to work at a firm where she had been for more than two years. She says that Wall Street has been slow to computerize, and she hates the necessary clerical work with each sales transaction. It's also tough to be responsible for other people's money when you have no control over the market. Her attraction to a career in selling stocks is the unlimited money she can make. "There's no ceiling on how much you can make," says Williams. "If you work hard and are smart, the sky's the limit in sales. I like the entrepreneurial spirit of sales," says Ann. "To a large extent, you're your own boss in this job, unlike a corporate job at the same level." She loves researching companies, reading annual reports, looking into businesses in every way she can. For example, the annual report of The Gap, a chain of retail stores, interested her, so she went to one of the stores to see for herself how many people were buying what. Williams loves the excitement of American business and working to learn more about how each one manages its profits.

What Education and Skills Will I Need?

High school: Preparation for college. Read the financial pages of newspapers in order to learn about financial situations, especially the business sections of the *New York Times* and the *Wall Street Journal*.

College: Almost all trainees for brokerage firms are college graduates. Most come from other careers—primarily professional or sales jobs.

Computer skills: Skill level 2—READ, ENTER. Stockbrokers have terminals on their desks to check constant changes in prices. They can call up clients' records, company information, and use the computer for other types of research.

Personal skills: Selling skills, interest in making money, love of finance and business, and ambition are needed for success in the stockmarket.

How Many Stockbrokers Are There and Where Do They Work?

There are 81,000 stockbrokers; only 20 percent are women and 4 percent black. They work for brokerage firms, investment banks, and mutual funds firms. Most work for a few large firms that have offices in large and small cities all over the United States.

How Much Money Will I Make?

Trainees start at $900 to $1,200 a month, depending on the size of the firm, until they are licensed and working on commission. In 1984, full-time stockbrokers who sold to individuals averaged $64,000 a year, while brokers selling to institutions averaged $156,000 a year.

What Are the Job Opportunities?

The job outlook is expected to be favorable through the 1980s. Jobs are always competitive, however. Merrill Lynch advises college graduates to get two or three years of successful business experience before they apply for a training program with a major investment firm.

Related Careers

Insurance finance   Securities trader
Real estate agent   Commodities broker

Where Can I Get More Information?

New York Stock Exchange
11 Wall Street
New York, New York 10005

Securities Industry Association
120 Broadway
New York, New York 10271
Send $1.00 for materials.

TRAVEL AGENT

Organizes, schedules, and sells travel
services to the public

What's It Like To Be a Travel Agent?

Travel agents are dealers in dreams—other people's dreams—
and in the course of a day they plan many around-the-world
trips, vacations, and special event trips, as well as the routine
business trips for regular customers. An agent must possess a
great deal of specialized knowledge about the climate, accom-
modations, fares, places of interest, tariffs and customs laws,
currency exchange, and sources of references for new information. When an anthropologist schedules a trip to Taute, New
Guinea, the agent must supply exact information about connections and time changes from airline to airline and time zone to
time zone. The agent must know that when the anthropologist
ends up in Lumi, walking through the bush is the only means
of transportation left to get from there to Taute. Travel agencies
are service agencies. Good will and good client relations are
vitally important to making a profit in these services. That's not
always easy, especially when a customer changes travel plans
for the sixth time! Knowing details, excursion rates, charters,
frequent flying deals, and suggestions for making trips conve-
nient and comfortable are imperative for a successful agent.

What Education and Skills Will I Need?

High school: Courses in geography, history, and a foreign language are helpful.
College: Most travel agents have some college background although it is not a requirement. Some travel agents take travel
agency courses that are offered in adult education classes, correspondence schools, community colleges, or private programs.
Others learn on the job, usually coming from other jobs.
Computer skills: Skill level 3—READ, ENTER, PRINT. Agents
use the computer most of the time to read schedules, enter ticket
information, and print tickets and billings to clients. Agents

learn these skills on the job, with special software programmed for the particular company.

Personal skills: Sales skills, business ability, interest in details and accuracy, and a pleasant personality that can accept people constantly changing their plans are necessary to be successful as a travel agent.

How Many Travel Agents Are There and Where Do They Work?

There are 72,000 full-time travel agents and many more who work part time and moonlight in order to get reduced travel fare benefits as well as commissions. Urban and resort areas have the most agents.

How Much Money Will I Make?

Entry level salaries are low, as the jobs are competitive and so many people want to work in the travel industry. In 1984, agents averaged from $10,000 to $20,000 a year. Owners of their own businesses make 5 percent on domestic travel, 10 percent on international travel, and 10 percent on cruises and hotels. Young people often go into this career for the fringe benefits, which include vacations at reduced rates, and transportation and hotels at a discount. Often, agents are invited for free holidays to see and recommend the facilities of an airline or resort hotel.

What Are the Job Opportunities?

The travel industry is one of the fastest growing fields and remains very competitive since it is one of the glamour careers that many qualified people apply for each year. The surest way to get a start in travel is to take any job a small agency offers you and work toward a promotion after learning the job. Another strategy for getting into the field is to bring in customers while you work another job, until you have impressed the boss enough for a full-time job.

Related Careers

Airline reservations agent   Tour guide
Salesperson

Where Can I Get More Information?

American Society of Travel Agents
4400 MacArthur Boulevard, NW
Washington, D.C. 20007

COMMUNICATIONS

ABOUT THESE CAREERS

Responses such as, "I'm a writer," or "I'm in TV," to the question, "What sort of work do you do?" almost always evoke envy. Communications careers are glamorous, and because they are, competition for most jobs is tough, with many more job seekers than there are job openings. Some people are attracted by the image of media jobs—the opportunities to meet public figures, to appear before nationwide audiences, to attend special events. It is often difficult to see the hard work required when looking at the glamorous aspects of communications careers.

The broadcasting business is undergoing a tremendous change, from three major networks to soaring numbers of independent stations on cable, a few by satellite, plus the VCR. The independents have increased to 250 stations; the numbers of households with cable increased from 29 million in 1982 to 41 million in 1985. Even more dramatic is the growth in VCRs, which are selling at the rate of almost 1 million a month, and are already in a quarter of the homes in the United States. With all the television choices, the average time a family spends watching the tube each week rose to 49 hours and 58 minutes in 1985—more than seven hours a day, seven days a week! Radio listening and advertising rates are up as well. Even though there are many more broadcasting jobs, it's as competitive as ever. For example, a major Boston radio station reports that it receives 5,000 résumés a year, and yet has only 20 openings.

The intellectual skills acquired at college are important for a communications career. Acute powers of observation and the ability to think clearly and logically are necessary traits, because people in communications need to understand the significance of the events they observe. A feeling for language enables newspaper reporters and broadcast journalists to breathe life and meaning into the overwhelming number of events that occur every day. A knack for drama through the spoken word makes radio and television announcers attractive to audiences of all kinds. Even though the competition is tough, there will be jobs through the 1980s for talented people who acquire appropriate education and experience. The business side is usually the easiest way to get into communications. Advertising sales, a very demanding job, is a common entry-level position. Another strategy is to find a small station hundreds of miles from a major city, maybe in the town or small city where you grew up, and be prepared to take any job that's available. A combination of talent, education, motivation, imagination, and luck is what you need.

CABLE TELEVISION

Plans, prepares, produces, and sells cable television programs

What's It Like To Be in Cable Television?

"You have to be hungry, ambitious, and energetic to compete in this industry," says Vivian Horner, vice-president of program development for Warner Amex Cable in New York. Cable television is the fastest growing communications career field in the country. When we think of television, the first jobs that come to mind are announcer and actor. But there are lots of other careers involved in setting up and running a cable system. Here are some of them: *Winning the franchise*—jobs include engineer, market analyst, financial analyst; *Building the system*—jobs include engineer and electronics and satellite technicians; *Running the system*—jobs include electrical engineer, sales specialist, marketing and advertising directors; *Programming and production*—jobs include director of public access, director of local origin programs, studio manager, sound and lighting technicians, newswriter.

After graduation from Oberlin, Mark Irish headed for New York City's cable TV world and landed a programming and production job at Showtime. His whole life is wrapped up in his work, which often keeps him in the office until 7 or 8 p.m., followed later in the evening by a film screening where "everyone" in the industry has to be seen. "A social life is almost impossible unless you take your date to work to the screenings," says Irish. "This life is just as crazy and glamorous and tough as they say it is. I love it. I wouldn't be anywhere else—except Los Angeles, doing the same thing."

What Education and Skills Will I Need?

High school: Preparation for college, with as much writing, speaking, and reading as you can get.

College: Major in communications, electronics engineering, radio and television, journalism, theater arts, business, or liberal arts.

Computer skills: Skill level 2—READ, ENTER. Planning and producing TV programs require using the computer for scheduling, budgets, and so on.

Personal skills: Programming careers required an interest in business, a lot of hustle, and interest in detail. The entertainment side of cable requires a well-modulated speaking voice, a reasonable command of the English language, plus knowledge of dramatics, sports, music, and current events.

How Many Cable Television Workers Are There and Where Do They Work?

There are 80,000 jobs in the system level of the cable TV industry and the jobs are clustered around major cities. Cable employment projections are that the current number will more than double in the late 1980s.

How Much Money Will I Make?

Members of a franchise team for a major cable TV company make from $25,000 to $40,000 a year. Selling is an important job in cable, as subscriber fees are the major source of income. Entry-level salaries range from $12,000 to $20,000 in sales, depending on geographic location. Experienced account executives can earn over $30,000. Operations is the business-management side of the TV industry. An operations manager oversees capital expenditures, customer service, accounts payable, installation and maintenance, and other administrative functions. Salaries for entry-level operations range from $12,000 to $15,000 in small systems and go over $20,000 in major cities.

What Are the Job Opportunities?

Along with computers, cable television and VCRs are the fastest growing industries of the 1980s. Like other communications fields, it is glamorous and there are many talented, ambitious young people applying for the jobs. Working in a ground-level industry is a wonderful opportunity to learn and grow with the industry.

Related Careers

Commercial and public
  radio
Commercial and public
  television
Business management
Sales

Where Can I Get More Information?

Cable Television Association
1724 Massachusetts Avenue, NW
Washington, D.C. 20036

The Cable Television Information Center
1500 North Beauregard Street, Suite 205
Alexandria, Virginia 22311

RADIO AND TELEVISION BROADCASTING

**Plans, prepares, produces, and presents
radio and television programs**

What's It Like To Be in Radio and Television Broadcasting?

The glamour and excitement of radio and television make broadcasting careers attractive to about 200,000 people who are employed in this career. Whether in commercial or public broadcasting, *radio and television directors* plan and supervise individual programs or series of programs. They coordinate the shows, select artists and studio personnel, schedule and conduct rehearsals, and direct on-the-air shows. They are often assisted by entry-level associates who arrange details, distribute scripts and changes in scripts to the cast, and help direct shows. They also may arrange for props, makeup service, artwork and film slides, and help with timing. *Announcers* are probably the best known workers in the industry. They introduce programs, guests, and musical selections and deliver most of the live commercials. In small stations, they also may operate the control board, sell time, and write commercial and news copy. *Musical directors*, following general instructions from program directors, select, arrange, and direct music for programs. News gathering and reporting are other key aspects of radio and television programming. *News directors* plan and supervise all news and special events coverage. *News reporters* gather and analyze information about newsworthy events for broadcast on radio or TV programs. They may specialize in a particular field, such as economics, health, or foreign affairs, and often report special news events from the scene. *Newswriters* select and write copy for newscasters to read on the air. In many stations, the jobs of newswriter and newscaster are combined. In addition, broadcasting stations have video and film editors, engineering technicians, a sales department that sells time to advertisers that sponsor the programs, and a general administration department.

Two disc jockeys, one on the East Coast and the other on the West Coast, have a lot in common. Both Peter Standish and Tammy Heide started volunteering for their college radio stations in their first college year. By the time they graduated, they had four years of experience and a lot of contacts. Peter had been working on the campus radio station, as an intern for a music trade publication, and for KQAK, a leading radio station in San Francisco, all at the same time. Even with the contacts, Tammy and Peter are quick to point out that you need a lot of luck to get the breaks in this competitive job market. They've worked hard and been lucky. They wouldn't change anything unless it was a little more music history and liberal arts while they were in college.

What Education and Skills Will I Need?

High school: Preparation for liberal arts college or a communications major, with as much writing, speaking, and reading as you can get in high school.

College: Major in liberal arts, communications, radio and television, journalism, theater arts, or a related area. Most broadcasters have been working part time in related jobs while in college.

Computer skills: Skill level 2—READ, ENTER. Broadcasting careers require the minimum skills, although word processing is useful.

Personal skills: Announcers must have a pleasant and well-controlled voice, good timing, excellent pronunciation, and good grammar. The videotaped audition that presents samples of an applicant's delivery, style, and appearance often is the most important factor in hiring. Programming careers require an interest in business and details as well.

How Many Radio and Television Workers Are There and Where Do They Work?

There are 56,000 announcers and newscasters and 120,000 full-time and 30,000 part-time staff employed in commercial broadcasting; half are in radio. They work in 7,000 commercial radio stations and 700 commercial television stations in the United States. In addition, there are 700 educational radio stations and 220 educational television stations. There are also 3,150 cable TV systems that hire about 9,500 workers.

How Much Money Will I Make?

Salaries in broadcasting vary widely with the type of station, the size of the market it serves, and with the announcer's popularity.

In 1984, radio announcers made from $12,000 to $33,000 a year. Television broadcasters made from $12,800 to $182,000 a year, with much higher salaries going to the very few major TV newscasters.

What Are the Job Opportunities?

Radio and television broadcasting are two very popular careers. The professional-level jobs are highly competitive, and thousands of liberal arts graduates apply for the few jobs available every spring. The small local stations are the least competitive and offer the beginner the most valuable diverse experience in communications. The chances for jobs are best with radio because there are many more of them and they hire more beginners.

Related Careers

Commercial and public
    radio
Commercial and public
    television

Cable television

Where Can I Get More Information?

National Association of Broadcasters
1771 North Street, NW
Washington, D.C. 20036

WRITER

**Writes clear and meaningful copy for
newspapers, magazines, books, technical
and trade brochures, and advertising**

What's It Like To Be a Writer?

A newspaper editor for a small city paper processes copy, writes
stories, puts on headlines, marks pictures, dummies pages,
checks Teletypesetters and composition, opens stacks of mail,
and answers the phone, which rings constantly. A daily newspaper has a fast pace and a deadline atmosphere not found in
other writing jobs. Beginning reporters are assigned civic, club,
and police—court proceedings. As they gain experience, they
may report more important events. Reporters may advance to
reporting for larger papers or press services. Magazine writers
write features or are researchers, interviewers, and coauthors.
Magazine production is similar to newspaper production in that
both are dependent upon advertising for profits. Magazine personnel work closely with their advertising agency. The pace on
a magazine is faster than that of book publishing because magazines have weekly or monthly deadlines. Fashion writers write
about fashion for department stores, trade publications, advertising agencies, and newspaper columns. Radio and TV newswriters put the news into short sentences for listening purposes.
The major networks have staffs of writers for their newscasts.
Technical writers rewrite technical and scientific articles for use
by nontechnical people or people in other scientific fields. Freelance writers work independently in a wide variety of subject
areas. Andrew Potok, author of the book *Ordinary Daylight*,
says, "What I like best about writing is the opportunity to sit
and think and spin tales. It's an incredible privilege to lock
yourself up in a room and plumb the depths to spin those tales.
That's not to say it's easy and goes well. It's terribly difficult,
as self-discipline and interior work always are. Still, I am always
awed by the privilege I have of spending my life writing."

What Education and Skills
Will I Need?

High school: Preparation for college, with as much language
skill and experience as you can get. Any part-time or summer

work on a local newspaper will help you find out what some writing jobs are like. Work on as many school publications as you can while in high school.

College: Writers come from journalism, English, and liberal arts majors, and from a great variety of programs. Most commercial writers have college degrees; however, college is not a neccessity for success as a writer. Writing and communications skills, together with a special style and interesting experiences, are what count.

Computer skills: Skill level 5—READ, ENTER, PRINT, SELECT, GRAPHICS. Every writer who can afford it uses a word processor, and many use graphics in their work.

Personal skills: Writing skills, imagination, curiosity, resourcefulness, an accurate memory, and ability to work alone or in a bustling environment are all necessary for most writing jobs.

How Many Writers Are There and Where Do They Work?

There are 69,000 reporters and correspondents; 76 percent work for newspapers and 14 percent work for broadcasting. There are 20,000 technical writers in electronics and aerospace industries, and most are men. There are about 191,000 writers and editors, of whom 22 percent work for newspaper and book companies, 16 percent work for business services, and 8 percent work for membership organizations. Most of the book publishing jobs are in New York City, while newspaper jobs are throughout the country, where smaller and special-interest newspapers are flourishing.

How Much Money Will I Make?

In 1984, newspaper reporters who worked under union contracts started at $300 to $450 a week. Reporters with experience made from $400 to $843 a week, with the top reporters for the major big city papers bringing home over $60,000 a year. Experienced book editors made from $21,000 to $31,000 a year. Technical writers started at $19,000 and made up to $31,000 with experience. Supervisors averaged $45,900 a year. A few book editors who work with bestselling authors made over $50,000 a year. Like most performing artists, most book writers cannot make a living with their craft. Writers often teach, work in publishing, or have other jobs to supplement their writing income.

What Are the Job Opportunities?

The writing jobs in urban centers are competitive. Thousands of English and journalism majors look for writing jobs each year in New York and other major cities. Every bit of experience counts. If you can publish while in college, or work in a writing job during the summer, you will have a head start on the competition. Best chances for newspaper jobs are in smaller towns and with special-interest papers. Most technical writers start working in that field after several years' experience in technology or engineering.

Related Careers

Journalist	Nonfiction writer
Translator	Biographer
Copywriter	Screenwriter
Fiction writer	

Where Can I Get More Information?

American Newspaper Publishers Association
The Newspaper Center, Box 17407
Dulles International Airport
Washington, D.C. 20041

National Newspaper Association
1627 K Street, NW
Suite 400
Washington, D.C. 20006

American Society of Magazine Editors
575 Lexington Avenue
New York, New York 10022

Society for Technical Communications
815 15th Street, NW
Suite 506
Washington, D.C. 20005

Women in Communications
PO Box 9561
Austin, Texas 78766

EDUCATION

ABOUT THESE CAREERS

Education careers require more education for less pay and, except for elementary school, have the bleakest outlook for job opportunities than any other career group. The oversupply of teachers graduating each year from college, the decrease in funding for education, the decreased enrollment in school (except for elementary education, which started to increase in 1985), and the closing down of many federally sponsored programs have made this field very competitive.

There are 2.5 million teachers plus professors and librarians represented by the descriptions in this section, and all the jobs require a college education. Most require a master's degree or a doctorate for professional certification or promotion.

Every state offers an education major in its state college or university. Write to the Department of Education in your state and inquire which schools offer this major. If you choose to go to a liberal arts college, there are several options for certification in elementary and secondary education, including summer school, a master's degree program, and correspondence courses.

If education is the field for you, your best bet is to specialize in elementary, vocational and technical education, bilingual education, mathematics and science, or education for the disabled or disadvantaged. The computer industry has been draining education's potential supply of mathematics teachers and therefore the biggest demand in public schools and colleges is for teachers of mathematics. Times are changing though, and by 1995, high school enrollments are predicted to increase, providing a new outlook for young educators.

COLLEGE PROFESSOR

Provides instruction for students in college-
level learning

What's It Like To Be a College Professor?

"College teaching is not an occupation but a way of life. The involvement with the subject you are teaching, the reading of professional literature in your field, and the discussions with students and colleagues become your point of view for living," writes Gail Bucknell, Associate Professor of Economics at Northwestern University. College professors who teach full time average 8 to 12 hours a week in the classroom. Higher-ranked professors who advise graduate students and are actively engaged in research may spend only 4 to 6 hours a week in actual classroom teaching. Outside the classroom, much of a professor's time is spent preparing for teaching, grading student work, and keeping up with the subject matter. Most professors carry on research projects and write for professional journals. Summers may be spent teaching summer school, doing research projects, or on vacation. Roberto Chavey, a Texas professor married to a professor, says that the lifestyle of two college professors can make a most interesting family life: "We take turns tending our children and sharing the domestic work as most of our career time is flexible and a lot of our professional work can be done at home."

What Education and Skills Will I Need?

High school: Preparation for college, with as strong an academic program as you can handle well.
College: Preparation for graduate school in whatever major you show the most ability and interest. Your graduate work doesn't have to be in the same field as your undergraduate work, although it is usually related. As you learn more about your academic abilities and interests, your major field may change. Plan to get your Ph.D. if you want to be a college professor.
Computer skills: Skill level 4—READ, ENTER, PRINT, SELECT.

Most professors use a word processor for their research and writing.

Personal skills: Professors need to be curious about learning, and able to share their enthusiasm and interest in their subject with their students. They must like detail and be persistent in order to follow through on academic research and writing.

How Many Professors Are There and Where Do They Work?

There are 731,000 college professors; 36 percent are women and 5 percent are black. Half of all college professors are employed in eight states, each with college enrollment exceeding two million: California, Illinois, Massachusetts, Michigan, New York, Ohio, Pennsylvania, and Texas.

How Much Money Will I Make?

In 1984, the average salary for a nine-month contract for a college instructor was $19,500; for an assistant professor, $24,600; for an associate professor, $25,300; and for a full professor, $39,900. Beginning salaries are much less than the average.

What Are the Job Opportunities?

College teaching will remain very competitive through the 1980s with decreasing college enrollments and increasing numbers of Ph.D.s looking for jobs. The largest number of jobs will be in science and engineering. Adult education is the other best bet for jobs.

Related Careers

College administrator   Writer
Government research   Librarian

Where Can I Get More Information?

American Association of University Professors
1 Dupont Circle
Suite 5000
Washington, D.C. 20036

COLLEGE STUDENT PERSONNEL

**Helps students meet their personal, social,
housing, and recreational needs**

What's It Like To Be in Student Personnel?

Student personnel staff are responsible for individualizing education for college students. This includes counseling students; advising student government officers; overseeing residence hall programs and orientation programs for new students; supervising fraternities and student honoraries; and communication between faculty and students. All these activities become very meaningful when working with students to try to enable them to take advantage of all their educational opportunities. Marc Freidman, Director of Student Personnel in a college of liberal arts in the Northwest, encourages people to go into college personnel if they like the academic style of life, and if they have a commitment to education and students. Adult students, who often combine family life or single parenthood with student life and a job, have concerns different from those of younger students. College personnel also work with the special needs of off-campus students.

What Education and Skills Will I Need?

High school: Preparation for college, with a broad range of academic subjects.

College: Many students prepare for graduate school with a major in social sciences or education. A master's degree is required for student personnel in higher education, and a doctorate is required for the bigger universities and top career jobs.

Computer skills: Skill level 5—READ, ENTER, PRINT, SELECT, GRAPHICS. Computer skills are needed for scheduling events, keeping track of housing, courses, and career data, and making presentations.

Personal skills: The ability to work with people of all backgrounds and ages; emotional stability while under pressure from students, parents, and faculty; and patience when working with conflicting viewpoints are necessary skills in college personnel.

How Many College Personnel Workers Are There and Where Do They Work?

There are 50,000 college student personnel workers; about half of them are women and 13 percent are black. The jobs they hold include dean of men, dean of women, dean of students, director of admissions, residence hall dean, registrar, counselor, financial aid officer, foreign student adviser, student union worker, student government specialist, and activities director. Every two-year and four-year college in the country hires student personnel workers.

How Much Money Will I Make?

In 1984, the median salary of student personnel workers was $22,600 a year. Beginners started at around $19,000.

What Are the Job Opportunities?

Competition for work in student personnel is expected through the 1980s because of decreasing college enrollments, especially among residential students.

Related Careers

High school counselor   Industrial personnel
School psychologist   manager
School administrator

Where Can I Get More Information?

American College Personnel Association
Two Skyline Place, 5203 Leesburg Pike
Falls Church, Virginia 22041

EARLY CHILDHOOD EDUCATOR

Instructs children from two through five
years old; day-care workers take
responsibility for infants as well

What's It Like To Be an Early Childhood Educator?

An early childhood educator works with small groups of children in an unstructured situation for a few hours a day. The program usually consists of reading to the children, painting, working with clay and crafts, free play, music, dance, teaching colors and numbers, and talking about community services, transportation, and families. Day-care and child-care centers often run from 7:00 a.m. until 7:00 p.m.; children come and go according to the hours their parents work. As more two-career families send their preschool children to these centers, jobs increase for professionals in this crucial field. Day-care director Mary Marshall says, "You learn how delightful human beings can be when you work with young children as they learn, are curious, and show their many interests. Early childhood education is just beginning to get the recognition it deserves for its importance in child development." Kevin Seifert, teacher at the demonstration preschool at San Jose State University, says that male teachers in a child-care center face special problems in that children often mistrust a man in this role. According to Seifert, most male child-care workers work part time and don't remain long in the field—often just long enough to get experience for an administrative job in early education.

What Education and Skills Will I Need?

High school: Preparation for college.
College: You can prepare for early childhood education with a two-year program in a community college, or a degree program in a four-year college, or an advanced degree. Most nursery

schools are private, and a degree is not required for teaching. Many nursery schools are informal cooperatives where the children's parents are involved in teaching and planning school programs. Day-care centers and government programs for early childhood education increasingly will require degrees; master's degrees will be necessary for the administration of these programs.

Computer skills: Skill level 2—READ, ENTER. Most educators need to read a terminal and enter student information.

Personal skills: Ability to be firmly low-keyed to allow children to express themselves in a learning environment; an avid interest in the growth and development of small children; and the ability to be relaxed in an active setting.

How Many Early Childhood Educators Are There and Where Do They Work?

Ninety percent of the 259,000 nursery and kindergarten teachers are women. Most communities have several nursery schools and day-care centers.

How Much Money Will I Make?

Like all "women's work," the pay is exceedingly low—even for college graduates. Salaries vary more than any other teaching job because the school may be in a parent's home, or a private business, or an organized chain of schools. If the job is in the public school system, teachers are paid the same as elementary school teachers, who have beginning salaries of around $14,000.

What Are the Job Opportunities?

The job opportunities will be improving as enrollment of early childhood programs increases with the baby boom, and as women continue to work full time. A shortage of teachers for this age level is expected through the 1980s.

Related Careers

Elementary school teacher   Salesperson
Librarian   Personnel

Where Can I Get More Information?

National Association for the Education
    of Young Children
1834 Connecticut Avenue, NW
Washington, D.C. 20009

ELEMENTARY SCHOOL TEACHER

**Teaches science, mathematics, language,
and social studies to children in
kindergarten through sixth grade**

What's It Like To Be an Elementary School Teacher?

Robert Braun, with twenty years' experience in business and technology, shares a fifth-grade teaching job with Elise Braun, his wife. He doesn't know of one male who has spent a lifetime in elementary teaching. "Most try it for a few years, go back to school for administration, or switch to business as financial pressure mounts." Elementary teachers play a vital role in the development of children. They teach the basics of mathematics, language, science, and social studies. They try to instill good study habits and an appreciation for learning. Teachers observe and evaluate each child's performance and potential. In addition, teachers work outside the classroom preparing lessons and grading papers, and attend faculty and parent meetings after school. What is learned or not learned in these early years shapes children's views of themselves in the world, affecting later success or failure in school and work. Other than family, there is no more crucial influence on the growing child than the elementary school teacher.

What Education and Skills Will I Need?

High school: Preparation for college, with as broad a program as possible. Most elementary teachers teach all subjects, including music, art, and physical education. So, be prepared!

College: Four years of college with a major in elementary education is required. A teaching certificate is awarded by every state, and many states require a fifth year of preparation for a permanent certificate. Plan your fifth year or master's degree in a special area of education, such as administration.

Computer skills: Skill level 2—READ, ENTER. Even if you don't teach computer literacy to children, you will need the basics for reading a terminal and entering data.

Personal skills: Dependability, good judgment, creativity, and enthusiasm for the development of young children are needed.

How Many Elementary School Teachers Are There and Where Do They Work?

There are 1,366,000 teachers; only 18 percent are men and 11 percent are black. In addition, there are 60,000 principals and supervisors, who are mostly men. They teach school in every city, town, and village in America.

How Much Money Will I Make?

Salaries are determined by level of education, work experience, and the particular town in which a teacher is employed. Most states have a minimum of $14,000 to $18,000 for beginning teachers, and the average salary for all elementary teachers in 1985 was $23,092 for a ten-month contract.

Teachers' salaries are on the way up. They are unionized in most parts of the country; teachers in Michigan, for example, expect to start at $30,000 by 1990. Here are some of the state averages for public schools for 1985:

Alaska	$39,000	New Hampshire	$18,577
California	$26,000	Ohio	$22,737
Idaho	$19,700	Pennsylvania	$24,435
Mississippi	$15,971	Wyoming	$26,709

What Are the Job Opportunities?

Excellent! There is a shortage which is predicted to be a national crisis because of the increase in elementary school enrollment and decrease in education graduates starting in 1985 through the end of the decade.

Related Careers

School administrator   Salesperson
Training manager

Where Can I Get More Information?

American Federation of Teachers
555 New Jersey Avenue, NW
Washington, D.C. 20001

HIGH SCHOOL TEACHER

Teaches a specific subject in junior or senior high school, grades 7 through 12

What's It Like To Be a High School Teacher?

High school teachers instruct four or five classes a day and supervise study halls, lunch, and extracurricular activities. If you're a high school student now, or have recently graduated, you have a good idea of what a high school teacher does because you've had a chance to observe teachers at work and interact with them. You certainly have noticed which ones enjoy their work, which ones make the most sense to you, and what their lives are like.

John Slayton, a high school teacher working abroad for the United States Department of Defense, has taught military dependents in Japan and Turkey and is currently teaching in

Holland. He loves living in an apartment in a nearby Dutch village rather than on the military base where he teaches. Slayton socializes with other American, Canadian, and British teachers, enjoying the advantage of living in a foreign country on an American salary. Slayton says the frustrating part of his work is not having a solution for handling the small group of students who disrupt the learning process of their classmates. What he likes best is the satisfaction of helping young people prepare for independent, successful careers in our increasingly complex world as they respond to what they learn about themselves. "Teaching," says Slayton, "is a daily challenge and a wonderful variety of experiences that the students continually offer."

What Education and Skills Will I Need?

High school: Preparation for college, with as broad a program as possible.

College: Major in the subject you wish to teach, or a related subject if you are planning to attend graduate school. Each state has its own certification system, and many require a master's degree for permanent certification. There are many ways for you to do graduate work, including summer school, evening school, and correspondence courses.

Computer skills: Skill level 2—READ, ENTER. Even if you don't teach or work with computers, you will need the basics to read the terminal and enter data about students.

Personal skills: Good teachers have a desire to work with young people, an interest in a special subject, and the ability to motivate others and to relate information to them.

How Many High School Teachers Are There and Where Do They Work?

There are over a million high school teachers; about half of them are women, and 7 percent are black. They work in every community in the United States.

How Much Money Will I Make?

Salaries vary with each community and with the teacher's educational background and experience. In 1985, the average salary for a high school teacher was $23,546 a year. Most states now have a minimum salary of $14,000 to $19,000 for a beginner with a bachelor's degree. See "Elementary School Teacher" for a partial list of average salaries by state.

What Are the Job Opportunities?

Competitive until after 1995, when enrollments in high schools are expected to boom. Until then, unless you teach mathematics or science, jobs will be tough to find.

Related Careers

School administrator   Public relations
Training manager   Salesperson

Where Can I Get More Information?

American Federation of Teachers
555 New Jersey Avenue, NW
Washington, D.C. 20001

LIBRARIAN

**Selects and organizes collections of books
and other media and provides access to
information**

What's It Like To Be a Librarian?

A librarian offers the services of getting books and other information to individuals and special groups, of educating the public about what is available, and of helping people of all ages to explore the wonderful world of books. The computer revolution has introduced the information explosion of the eighties. In large libraries many librarians specialize and have a single function, such as cataloging, publicity, reference work, or working with a special subject such as art, medicine, or science. *Public librarians* serve all kinds of readers; *school librarians* work only with the students and staff of their schools; and *university librarians* work with students, staff, and research workers. "Students planning a career as a school librarian should know what the job is like," says Elizabeth Dow, elementary school librarian. "It helps if one has a capacity for remembering trivia, a capacity for keeping a lot of loose ends in mind, and a sense of humor. Nobody else really understands the joy of discovering the perfect Dewey number for an item that has been nagging at your head. The part of the job that makes it all worthwhile is connecting the perfect library item with a student at the exact moment the student needs it. This could be the right story, item of information, or curiosity stimulator. Seeing the click in the children's eyes and knowing I've expanded their world or met their need is a great high."

What Education and Skills Will I Need?

High school: Preparation for college, with as broad a program as possible. It is important to develop language skills.

College: Strong liberal arts program to prepare for a graduate degree in library science. A reading knowledge of one foreign language is often required. Computer science is increasingly essential to the job.

Computer skills: Skill level 4—READ, ENTER, PRINT, SELECT. Librarians need to be computer proficient to use a data base for information gathering for research purposes.

Personal skills: Good librarians have a strong intellectual curiosity and an interest in helping others to use library materials.

How Many Librarians Are There and Where Do They Work?

There are 151,000 librarians; 83 percent are women and 7 percent are black. They work mostly for educational institutions (71 percent) and for local government (11 percent), usually as public librarians. In addition, there are another 7,800 audiovisual specialists working in libraries.

How Much Money Will I Make?

In 1984, a graduate school librarian started at $18,791 and a specialist started at $20,233 a year. Experienced school librarians averaged $23,173 a year, special librarians averaged $28,421, and college librarians averaged $26,000.

What Are the Job Opportunities?

The best chances are for specialized librarians in medicine, law, business, engineering, and science. Information management outside the traditional library setting is expected to offer excellent employment in industry and government agencies needing qualified people with computer skills.

Related Careers

Museum curator   Research analyst
Archivist

Where Can I Get More Information?

American Library Association
50 East Huron Street
Chicago, Illinois 60611

Special Libraries Association
1700 18th Street, NW
Washington, D.C. 20009

MUSEUM CAREERS

Creates museum exhibits and manages the
work of an art museum, a natural history
museum, or a historical or industrial
museum

What's It Like To Be in Museum Careers?

Directors and curators of a museum design and install exhibits, organize gallery talks and educational programs, acquire new art objects for the collections, and revise old exhibits. "Operations people are the landlords and superintendents of the building. They are in charge of temperature control, security, admissions, restaurants, installing and moving the exhibits, and preparing budgets for their programs," explains Lita Semerad, executive assistant to the vice-president of operations for The Metropolitan Museum of Art in New York. An art history major, she has been with the Metropolitan for twelve years. Semerad advises young people interested in a museum career to be ready to start at the bottom and take anything to get a start. She has helped many aspiring museum workers to get part-time jobs with a particular exhibit or project, which have often expanded into full-time work.

Curators search for, acquire, catalog, restore, exhibit, maintain, and store items of interest. In the Greek and Roman art department of New York's Metropolitan Museum is their youngest curator, Dr. Max Anderson. At 28, he is assistant curator, but his first job there was a summer job between college and graduate school. Since he started full time, Anderson got an edge on the competition through his language ability. He speaks fluent Italian, exactly what was needed during a recent Vatican exhibit. Because of that, he ended up traveling with the exhibit to Chicago and San Francisco. He also speaks French, German, and Spanish and reads Greek and Latin as well. Anderson, like other curators, knows that a job well done results in good attendance, good public relations, and increased revenue for the museum.

What Education and Skills Will I Need?

High school: Preparation for college, with emphasis on art and social sciences.

College: Most people in museum careers majored in art history, the classics, or anthropology. A few universities give graduate degrees in museum management. Most top management jobs go to the MBAs.

Computer skills: Skill level 5—READ, ENTER, PRINT, SELECT, GRAPHICS. Operations personnel need computer skills to organize the security system, prepare budgets, and present reports using graphics.

Personal skills: Creativity, an interest in history and art, and the ability to teach others is needed for success in museum careers.

How Many Museum Workers Are There and Where Do They Work?

There are 11,000 curators and archivists, with a total of about 30,000 professional museum workers. About 40 percent work for the government and 30 percent in private museums. Most curators in the federal government are employed by the Smithsonian and the military museums of the Department of Defense. Most curators work in the major cities where the large museums are—New York, Washington, Chicago, Los Angeles, and Boston.

How Much Money Will I Make?

In 1984, beginning curators with a master's degree averaged $26,400, and Ph.D.s started at an average of $31,600. Archivists get less than curators and MBAs in museum administration start at about the same.

What Are the Job Opportunities?

Very competitive. In spite of low pay (except in the National Gallery of Art, the Metropolitan in New York City and the Getty Museum in Los Angeles), most art history majors want to work in America's great museums, and many of them apply for the few museum openings each year. An advanced degree with some part-time or summer experience is the best chance for the new graduate to enter the field. Also, "getting hired part time by a project director, rather than going through personnel, often gets your foot in the door," advises Semerad of the Metropolitan.

Related Careers

Librarian
Anthropologist

Art designer
Archivist

Where Can I Get More Information?

American Association of Museums
1055 Thomas Jefferson Street, NW
Washington, D.C. 20007

PHYSICAL EDUCATION TEACHER

Teaches physical education and health to students from preschool through adult education

What's It Like To Be a Physical Education Teacher?

The physical education teacher gets to know the students well because sports and after-school activities offer an informal learning situation. They are often called upon to help other staff members, the guidance department, and the administration to know more about the behavior of a particular student. Teachers often plan their own physical education program, geared to the sports and activities in which they are interested, the interests of the community in which they teach, and the facilities available. There is a trend to include individual sports programs away from school, such as weekend skiing, biking, and backpacking. Dr. Natalie Shepard, professor of physical education, reminds college students that "this is not for you if you just live to play sports. It is an educational career, and sports are the medium for teaching students. Sports are one place where students can learn about leadership, aggression, and competition with everyone's approval."

What Education and Skills Will I Need?

High school: Preparation for college, with an emphasis on life sciences. Participate in as many sports as possible.

College: Major or minor in physical education. A master's degree is needed for certification in many states, and always for college teaching. Anatomy, physiology, and health courses are required for a physical education major. It helps to have summer work in recreation programs to get experience.

Computer skills: Skill level 2—READ, ENTER. This is the minimum needed to read the terminal and enter student data. Some coaches use the computer for scheduling games and planning game strategies, which requires more advanced skills.

Personal skills: Physical education teachers must be athletic, have an ability to encourage those who are not athletic, an interest in total development of students, a sense of fairness, and an ability to encourage youth toward good health.

How Many Physical Education Teachers Are There and Where Do They Work?

Every high school and most elementary schools have a physical education teacher. Summer recreational and administrative work are available with camps and playgrounds.

How Much Money Will I Make?

Salaries are the same as those of all teachers within a particular school system. In 1985, high school teachers averaged $24,276 a year.

What Are the Job Opportunities?

The best chances for jobs are in elementary schools, where enrollment has increased as of 1985. Secondary schools are in critical need of coaches, and physical education teachers will increasingly be in demand by 1990. Opportunities are also excellent in special education, inner-city schools, and rural areas.

Related Careers

Teacher   Athletic director
Coach   Athletic trainer

Where Can I Get More Information?

American Association of Health, Physical
   Education and Recreation
1201 16th Street, NW
Washington, D.C. 20036

SCHOOL ADMINISTRATOR

**Manages, directs, and coordinates the
activities of a school, college, or university**

What's It Like To Be a School Administrator?

Administrators manage schools and school systems. An important part of their job is to provide classroom teachers with the best possible environment in which to teach. Principals visit classrooms, review instructional objectives, evaluate teachers, and examine learning materials. They confer with the teachers and other staff, talk with parents, and meet with students. Their primary responsibility is to insure high-quality classroom instruction to the students. Milt Israel, an assistant superintendent of schools, says, "This job has grown more complex in recent years. The trend toward consolidation and answering the needs of many different vocal and often angry groups is hard work! Issues that confront most school administrators today include: quality education, desegregation, contract negotiations with teachers, spiraling costs, and taxpayer resistance to higher taxes. Not to mention after-school care of children with no parents at home, and health needs of children such as meals at school and now the AIDS scare among parents and children."

What Education and Skills Will I Need?

High school: Preparation for any college major that relates to teaching or education.

College: Major in any subject you wish to teach in school or college. If you want to be a college dean, college president, or superintendent of a large city high school, prepare for a master's degree and work toward your doctorate in administration.

Computer skills: Skill level 4—READ, ENTER, PRINT, SELECT. Administrators need computer skills for planning budgets, writing reports, and scheduling classes and events.

Personal skills: An interest in the development of students, business abilities, and the ability to communicate with many diverse people are necessary.

How Many School Administrators Are There and Where Do They Work?

There are 133,000 administrators; 36 percent are women and 12 percent are black. They work in every community in the country.

How Much Money Will I Make?

Administrators usually get paid some percentage more than the teachers earn in any school. A superintendent of a small school system, with a master's degree, earns about $20,000 a year, and a superintendent of a large school system, with a doctorate, earns $50,000 a year or more. In 1985, an elementary school principal averaged $36,452, a junior high school principal averaged $39,650, and a high school principal averaged $42,094 a year.

What Are the Job Opportunities?

The employment outlook is competitive as upper-division school enrollments decrease. The best chances are in elementary education where enrollment is expected to boom in the late 1980s.

Related Careers

Teacher

Management in business or government

Where Can I Get More Information?

American Association of School Administrators
1801 North Moore Street
Arlington, Virginia 22209

National Association of Secondary School
    Administrators
1904 Association Drive
Reston, Virginia 22091

SCHOOL COUNSELOR

Helps students understand their interests,
abilities, and personality characteristics in
the context of their educational decision
making

What's It Like To Be a School Counselor?

According to David Phau, school counselor in a Chicago suburban high school, "I spend half of my day with students, in-
dividually or in small groups; about a fourth of the day talking
with parents and teachers, on the phone and in conferences;
and the other fourth in administrative work, with records, college and work applications, and correspondence. After-school
hours also are important since students and teachers like to
drop by the guidance office informally with questions or for
visits. Many evenings are involved attending school activities.
It is important to the students to have their counselors attend
sports, social, and cultural activities." Counselors are responsible for helping students with their educational and career development. They provide students with information that helps
them to make informed, appropriate, and satisfying educational
choices. In this way, counselors provide students with a basis
for sound educational decision making.

What Education and Skills Will I Need?

High school: Preparation for college. Most school counselors
teach a subject before going into counseling.
College: A master's degree in guidance and one to five years of
teaching are required by most states to be a certified school
counselor. A doctorate is required for administrative careers in
guidance in big cities.
Computer skills: Skill level 3—READ, ENTER, PRINT. Many
counselors use computers for compiling a data base about colleges and careers; they plan schedules and programs on a
computer.

Personal skills: Successful counselors have an interest in helping others take responsibility for themselves, and an ability to work with other educators, parents, and students who may have varying opinions on student development.

How Many School Counselors Are There and Where Do They Work?

There are 148,000 counselors; half are women and about 13 percent are black. Most work in schools (61 percent), the others in social service agencies (18 percent) and in state government (13 percent).

How Much Money Will I Make?

Salaries vary with the school system, but usually counselors are paid more than classroom teachers and less than administrators. In 1985, the average salary for counselors was $27,593.

What Are the Job Opportunities?

All educational jobs, except in elementary schools, are competitive because of decreased enrollment. By 1990, secondary schools will also grow, providing counselors jobs on both levels. There are more student personnel graduates than job openings on the college level, although many of the people who became school counselors when there was a special demand for counselors 20 years ago, are retiring, providing increased openings in the late 1980s.

Related Careers

Psychologist   Social worker
Parole officer   Rehabilitation counselor

Where Can I Get More Information?

American School Counselor Association
Two Skyline Place, Suite 400
5203 Leesburg Pike
Falls Church, Virginia 22041

SPECIAL EDUCATION TEACHER

Teaches disabled children who are unable
to learn in large classroom situations
without special services; or teaches disabled
children who learn best when they are
separated into small groups

What's It Like To Be a Special Education Teacher?

Special education teachers spend their days assessing students
who have been referred for special education by classroom teachers, instructing children with disabilities in small groups, tutoring some children on a one-to-one basis, and supervising
teachers' aides. They spend a lot of time consulting with classroom teachers about the students who leave their classrooms
for tutoring but return to class and are "mainstreamed" most
of the school day. A special education teacher also evaluates
testing and is a regular team member for developing the Indi-
vidualized Educational Program (IEP) for children with disabilities. Pete Sinot, a special education teacher in Minnesota who
has a mentally retarded child of his own, says "Once I learned
to expect small accomplishments from the children, to slow
down and let the activities of the day go at a natural pace for
them, I was fine. Until then, I was uptight about achievement,
which caused anxiety and strife in the classroom." Sinot finds
his work very rewarding. He has learned to give what the student needs, rather than what he thinks the student needs.

What Education and Skills Will I Need?

High school: Preparation for college, with an emphasis on subjects that interest you.
College: Major in any subject, or in education, elementary education, or special education, and prepare for a master's degree.
Most states require a master's degree for certification, although
you can begin teaching with a bachelor's degree.

Computer skills: Skill level 2—READ, ENTER. All educators need to know how to read the terminal and enter student data.
Personal skills: Patience with slow progress, the ability to work with disabled children and their parents, and the ability to see accomplishment in things that might seem small compared to what you would normally expect.

How Much Money Will I Make?

Salaries vary with the community and the school system. They are the same as other teachers' salaries within the school system, averaging $24,276 a year with experience.

What Are the Job Opportunities?

The classified ads under "Education" are loaded with job opportunities for special education. Even though jobs depend upon federal funds to pay local school systems for providing special education, the minimum services needed are not being met.

Related Careers

Rehabilitation counselor
Social worker

Occupational therapist
Reading specialist

Where Can I Get More Information?

National Education Association
1201 16th Street, NW
Washington, D.C. 20036

GOVERNMENT

ABOUT THESE CAREERS

Government jobs offer the most security and least risk. The federal government is the nation's largest single employer. Even more people work for state and local governments. Altogether, one worker in every six is employed by the government, which provides about 16 million jobs! About 5 million of those workers are college graduates. The federal government's major function is defense; the next largest group of employees work for the postal service. Local governments regulate education, fire protection, hospitals, streets and highways, water and transit services. State government workers are in hospitals, on highways, in corrections, and public welfare.

Preparing for a career with the government is different from preparing for most career clusters because the government hires just about every kind of career described in this book. Therefore, accountants, physicians, teachers, nurses, and purchasing agents are all jobs that can be government careers. They require a great variety of educational backgrounds.

The government-related careers described in this career group, such as city manager, community planner, and lawyer, require graduate work. Volunteer jobs in the Peace Corps are limited to two years and do not necessarily lead to paying jobs that are directly related to that experience. Unless you are the top manager in your department, it is very difficult to bring about change through a government job. Rather than being motivated by profit or a desire to change the world, many people in government want to serve the public and have a direct impact on other people. And all government workers enjoy the fringe benefits including the best pension plan in the country.

CITY MANAGER

Administers and coordinates the day-to-day operations of the city

What's It Like To Be a City Manager?

Planning for future growth, dealing with air and water pollution, and controlling rising crime rates demand the services of a good city manager. City managers are also in charge of tax collection, law enforcement, public works, and preparing the city's budget. They are responsible to the community's elected officials who hire them. Besides attending to the daily activities of the city, they study long-range problems of traffic, housing, crime, and urban renewal and report their findings to the elected council. They often work with citizens' groups and give reports to special city committees. Many of the citizens' group meetings are held after regular work hours.

What Education and Skills Will I Need?

High school: Preparation for college, with group experience in as many school activities as interest you.
College: Major in business, engineering, recreation, or political science. A master's degree in public or municipal administration is necessary for the better jobs.
Computer skills: Skill level 4—READ, ENTER, PRINT, SELECT. Management careers require proficiency to analyze and present reports, and prepare the budget.
Personal skills: Ability to isolate problems quickly, identify their causes, and find solutions; good judgment; and self-confidence are needed for this job, as well as skills in working well with others.

How Many City Managers Are There and Where Do They Work?

There are 3,300 city managers plus many more assistant city managers and department heads. This is a new and growing career. Over three-quarters of the city managers work for small cities with populations of fewer than 25,000. There are almost no women in city management. Not until the past few years have women and blacks been elected mayors of major cities.

How Much Money Will I Make?

Starting salary for new college graduates was $19,000 a year for assistant city managers. In 1984, average salaries for experienced managers ranged from $33,000 a year in small cities to $80,000 in cities with populations over 500,000.

What Are the Job Opportunities?

Jobs will be competitive through the 1980s with many more graduates than jobs. The best opportunities are in the South and West.

Related Careers

Business manager   School administrator
Hospital administrator

Where Can I Get More Information?

International City Management Association
1140 Connecticut Avenue, NW
Washington, D.C. 20036

COMMUNITY PLANNER

**Develops plans and programs for orderly
growth and improvement of urban and
rural communities**

What's It Like To Be a Community Planner?

Alfred Lima has a college degree in landscape architecture and a master's degree in community planning. He started his own planning firm in Boston and spends a lot of time getting projects for his company. Right now his biggest project is one with the federal government—fire prevention in urban areas. Lima likes being his own boss and doing something useful and creative like preserving the urban environment. His usual work includes preparing a fire prevention master plan for the city, reviewing work completed by other staff members, and reading professional journals and publications. In addition, he works on basic studies such as data collection, economic base and regional analysis, population studies, map preparation; develops recommendations for land-use allocation, utilities, municipal facilities, housing, open spaces, and recreation and beautification programs; and plans implementation of budgets, subdivision regulations, and citizen information programs. Lima is a new stepfather to three young children but still must count on several evenings a week devoted to meetings with planning boards, civic groups concerned with planning, and professional meetings. He suggests that students learn the practical skills of graphics, drafting, and writing so they can do everything necessary to run a business.

What Education and Skills Will I Need?

High school: Preparation for college, with an emphasis on mathematics, computer science, and social science.
College: A beginning job requires a master's degree in urban or regional planning, which is offered in 80 colleges and universities. To prepare for graduate school, major in architecture, engineering, economics, social science, or public administration.
Computer skills: Skill level 5—READ, ENTER, PRINT, SELECT, GRAPHICS. Planners use computers for design of plans and for writing reports.
Personal skills: Ability to think in spatial relationships and to visualize plans and designs, flexibility in solving problems, and ability to cooperate with others who have different ideas are necessary qualities for planners.

How Many Community Planners Are There and Where Do They Work?

There are 17,000 community planners and about 10 percent are women. They work mostly for the government—73 percent for local government and 13 percent for state government. There has been an increase in management jobs in cities with populations of less than 50,000.

How Much Money Will I Make?

In 1985, the beginning salary for a planner with a master's degree working with the federal government was $21,800 a year. The average money for an experienced planner was $38,200. Consultants are paid on a fee basis, which is based on their regional or national reputation. Directors of planning earn an average salary of $44,400 a year.

What Are the Job Opportunities?

The employment outlook will become more competitive through the 1980s as the government spends less money for planning and graduates in planning increase. Geographic mobility is a must and a willingness to work in small towns or rural areas will help.

Related Careers

Architect   City manager
Planning engineer

Where Can I Get More Information?

American Planning Association
1776 Massachusetts Avenue, NW
Washington, D.C. 20036

FOREIGN SERVICE OFFICER

Serves in the overseas arm of the United States' foreign relations activities

What's It Like To Be a Foreign Service Officer?

Foreign service officers protect and promote the welfare and interest of the United States and its citizens. Working in the Department of State, they are responsible for advising the president on matters of foreign policy; for conducting relations with foreign countries; for protecting the political, economic, and commercial interests of the United States overseas; and for offering services to Americans abroad and to foreign nationals traveling to the United States. Genta A. Hawkins, a foreign service officer appointed by the president and confirmed by the Senate, tells about her first assignment. "As consular officer, I issued visas to tourists, diplomats, and businesspeople coming to the United States; helped Americans in distress; witnessed marriages; signed birth certificates; and renewed passports. When I was a member of the economic section, I traveled extensively throughout the Ivory Coast to find worthwhile projects and to assess their progress. I served as escort officer for a group of American journalists, and for an American folk group who toured the country. Most evenings were filled with official obligations. Dinners and diplomatic receptions were held at the beautiful presidential palace. My current assignment in Washington consists of writing speeches and articles, planning conferences, and acting as a liaison with private agencies. The evening responsibilities of a young foreign service officer in Washington are not as rigorous as in the field, but there are occasional receptions at the embassies and welcoming ceremonies on the White House lawn for visiting heads of states."

What Education and Skills Will I Need?

High school: Preparation for college, with emphasis in the social sciences, history, government, and foreign languages.

College: Foreign service officers come from liberal arts colleges, with majors in English, foreign languages, international relations, history, government, economics, or law. A master's degree is not a requirement, but most officers do have an advanced degree. Of the junior officers appointed, 54 percent had master's degrees, 11 percent had law degrees, and 6 percent had doctorates. Their ages ranged from the early twenties to the middle fifties, with a median age around 31, and most had a few years of professional experience. Some 45 percent possessed skills in one foreign language, and 7 percent had skills in two or more foreign languages. Everyone applying for an appointment must take the written examination, which is given once each year in December, in about 150 cities. Applications must be made by late October. In order to take the examination, you must be 20 years old, a United States citizen, and available for worldwide assignment.

Computer skills: Skill level 2—READ, ENTER. Minimum is to be able to read a terminal, although most officers will use a word processor.

Personal skills: Representatives of the United States government must have a good physical appearance, be tactful, and have a pleasant personality, as well as the ability to study and solve problems.

How Many Foreign Officers Are There and Where Do They Work?

There are 4,000 foreign service posts in Washington and in foreign countries and only 560 (14.8 percent) are filled by women. Foreign service officers serve as administrative, consular, economic, and political officers in more than 230 United States embassies and consulates in over 140 nations.

How Much Money Will I Make?

In 1985, beginning salaries ranged from $20,142 to $40,834, depending on education and experience. The top salary for experienced officers is the same for all federal employees, $67,940. In addition, there are many fringe benefits.

Related Careers

International business sales   Civil service
Import business

Where Can I Get More Information?

Board of Examiners for the Foreign Service
Box 9317, Rosslyn Station
Arlington, Virginia 22209

FEDERAL CIVIL SERVICE

**Federal government jobs represent every
kind of job found in private employment**

What's It Like To Be in Federal Civil Service?

Four-year college graduates can enter career management, administrative and personnel management, and technical and professional jobs with the government. Two-year college graduates can enter technical assistance careers in economics, administration, writing, data processing, finance, accounting, law, library science, and physical science.

There are two ways to get a federal job. The first and most common is by taking the civil service examination and being placed on a civil service register. Whenever a job opening occurs in a federal agency, the registers are scanned and the names of the best-qualified applicants are sent to the agency. You can increase your chances of getting a federal job by filling in more than one category and by agreeing to move anywhere in the country. The biggest barrier for women is the veteran's preference policy.

The second way to get a federal job is by political appointment. By law, there are over 3,000 high-level jobs that are filled in this way. If you are well known in your field, get in touch with your senator for a recommendation, or with your company for the President's Program for Executive Exchange. If you have not yet made a name for yourself in your career, working long and hard on a successful presidential campaign is another potential route to a high-level federal job. After three years of work in government service, the civil service worker has career status. For example, parents who leave a job to raise children can return to the same job level rather than competing again.

What Education and Skills Will I Need?

High school: Preparation for community college, business college, health training, or four-year college in any field that interests you.

College: The more education you have, the higher the career level open to you. Two-year college graduates take the Junior Federal Assistant Examination or the Junior Engineer and Science Assistant Examination to qualify for trainee-level positions for careers.

Computer skills: Skill level 2—READ, ENTER. All jobs would require the minimum skills.

Personal skills: Skills needed vary according to the career you select.

How Many Federal Civil Service Workers Are There and Where Do They Work?

Each year, ten thousand federal jobs requiring college degrees are filled and two-thirds of them go to men. In 1985, the federal government employed nearly 2 million white-collar workers. About 150,000 of them work in engineering, 150,000 in accounting, 120,000 in health service, and 45,000 in biological and agricultural science. One in eight federal employees works in Washington, D.C.; the remainder work all over the United States and abroad.

How Much Money Will I Make?

Salaries are paid according to the General Schedule (GS) and are set by Congress. The pay scale is set for all government employees in the professions, administrative jobs, and technical and clerical jobs. There are raises within each grade and increases are periodic for each grade. In 1985, graduates of a four-year college started at $14,700 or $17,800 a year, a person with a master's degree began work at $21,800, and experienced professionals averaged $36,000. The top was $67,940.

What Are the Job Opportunities?

The current political talk is to cut federal jobs. With our huge national deficit and budget-cutting trend come competition for government jobs. The chances for a position depend a lot on which career field interests you.

Related Careers

State government   Post office
Local government   Military

Where Can I Get More Information?

U.S. Civil Service Commission
Washington, D.C. 20415

HEALTH AND REGULATORY INSPECTOR

**Checks compliance with federal health,
safety, trade, and employment laws**

What's It Like To Be a Health and Regulatory Inspector?

There is a great variety of jobs for health and regulatory inspectors, such as food and drug inspector, meat and poultry inspector, agriculture quarantine inspector, sanitarian, commodity grader, immigration inspector, customs inspector, aviation safety officer, mine inspector, wage-hour compliance officer, and alcohol, tobacco, and firearms inspector. Inspector Paula Rakowski, in her twenties, inspects cars, buses, trains, and planes crossing the American–Canadian border. What she likes least about the job is the offensive attitude some people have toward being inspected by a woman. Often, people who are denied admission to the United States are abusive in their language and make physical threats, and they resent a woman having the authority to refuse them. What Rakowski likes best about the job is the shift work, which gives her a great variety of days and hours and people to work with. She also likes the interesting people she meets from all over the world.

What Education and Skills Will I Need?

High school: Preparation for community college or four-year college.
College: Most inspectors have two to four years of college plus specialized work experience related to the job they seek.
Computer skills: Skill level 2—READ, ENTER. Many inspectors have to enter data on a specialized program.
Personal skills: Inspectors must be responsible, good at detailed work, neat, and have good speaking skills.

How Many Health and Regulatory Inspectors Are There and Where Do They Work?

There are 101,000 inspectors; 15 percent are women and 7 percent are black. All work for the government—36 percent for the federal government, 34 percent for state government, and 26 percent for local government.

How Much Money Will I Make?

Following are some specific average salaries for experienced health and regulatory inspectors with the federal government: postal—$42,200; transportation—$42,100; coal mine—$35,800; civil rights—$34,600; and customs—$26,700.

What Are the Job Opportunities?

Chances for jobs will be fair through the 1980s. Little growth is expected, and most jobs will come from replacement.

Related Careers

Construction inspector   Law enforcement

Where Can I Get More Information?

Interagency Board of U.S. Civil Service Examiners
1900 E Street, NW
Washington, D.C. 20415

LAWYER

**Interprets laws, rulings, and regulations
for individuals and businesses**

What's It Like To Be a Lawyer?

Lawyers, also called attorneys, are involved in such diverse activities as defending or prosecuting people accused of crimes, granting patents, drawing up business contracts, advising clients on tax matters, settling labor disputes, and administering wills. Whether acting as advocates or advisers, they are all involved with in-depth research into the purposes behind certain laws. They study judicial decisions that have applied those laws to circumstances similar to those currently faced by the lawyer. Lawyers write reports or briefs that must communicate clearly and precisely. As our laws grow more complex, lawyers take on regulatory tasks in areas such as transportation, energy conservation, consumer protection, and social welfare.

Bill McDermit, married to his law partner, says there are certain activities that most lawyers do. Whether representing the defendant in a divorce case or the suing party (plaintiff) in a lawsuit, the lawyer has to know the relevant laws and the facts in the case to determine how the law affects the facts. Based on this determination, the lawyer decides what action is in the best interests of his client. Lawyers must know both legal and nonlegal matters. For example, divorce lawyers read about the changing role of the family in modern society, the different acceptable living arrangements, and the great variety of ways to live and love together. Most lawyers consult with clients to determine the details of problems, to advise them of the law, and to suggest action that might be taken. "Working in our own practice," reports McDermit, "gives us the kind of work and lifestyle we want together. We will not have children until we get this practice going, and maybe not even then. We work hard, and when we're finished, we really love to take off and have our time for sports and sun with no other worries or commitments."

What Education and Skills Will I Need?

High school: Preparation for college, with as much liberal arts and verbal and language skills as possible.

College: Prelaw graduates go to one of the 173 approved three-year law schools; then they must pass the bar examination in the state in which they will practice. English, literature, history, government, economics, philosophy, and social sciences are important in prelaw. An understanding of society and its institutions is required for law. About one-fifth of all law students attend part time, usually night school.

Computer skills: Skill level 3—READ, ENTER, PRINT. Lawyers are increasingly using computers for routine legal papers and reports, as well as using specialized data bases for their research.

Personal skills: Integrity and honesty are vital. Perseverance and reasoning ability are essential to analyze complex cases and reach sound conclusions. Creativity is necessary to handle unique problems.

How Many Lawyers Are There and Where Do They Work?

There are 490,000 lawyers; 15 percent are women and 3 percent are black. Most (60 percent) work for law firms or in business; 12 percent work for local government and 7 percent for federal. In 1981 Sandra Day O'Connor became the first female lawyer ever to serve as United States Supreme Court Justice. Her presence enables other women to aspire to this esteemed, prestigious, top position in law.

How Much Money Will I Make?

In 1984, the average beginning salary for a new graduate hired by a law firm was from $15,000 to $40,000 a year. The federal government started law school graduates at $21,800 to $26,400 in 1985. The average salary of the most experienced lawyers in private industry was $88,000, one of the top ten highest paid careers in the country.

What Are the Job Opportunities?

The first hurdle is getting into law school, which is highly competitive because of the increase in applicants since the seventies. Many graduates never practice law but use their legal education as a background for other jobs. Others apply their legal knowledge to human rights activities such as protecting and expanding women's and minority rights, arguing environmental and consumer cases, providing legal aid, and testing compliance with existing civil rights laws.

Related Careers

Negotiator   FBI special agent
Judge   Political office holder
Corporate manager   Lobbyist
Legislator

Where Can I Get More Information?

The American Bar Association
750 North Lake Shore Drive
Chicago, Illinois 60611

Association of American Law Schools
1 Dupont Circle, NW, Suite 370
Washington, D.C. 20036

MILITARY CAREERS

Members serve in the armed forces

What's It Like To Be in the Military?

In peacetime, it's like getting paid for job training and work experience. There are over 200 job-training courses in the army for technical, medical, communications, and electronics jobs that you can choose *before* you enter the service. The job you get depends on your present level of education and achievement. Each service has its own jobs, its own job training, and its own educational programs. Check with the army, the air force, the navy, the coast guard, and the marine corps for specific details. You can enlist in a variety of combinations of active and reserve duty. Active duty ranges from two to six years, with three-year and four-year enlistments most common.

What Education and Skills Will I Need?

High school: Required for enlisted personnel. Preparation for college in any major to qualify for the officers' training programs. In 1984, 94 percent of all military were high school graduates.

College: Your major in college qualifies you for the job you wish to select in the service. The military can use any and all types of skills and educational achievement.

Computer skills: It depends on your career choice.

Personal skills: It depends on your career choice.

Other qualifications: You must be between 18 and 27 years old, a United States citizen, and in good physical condition. There is no restriction on marital status, but you cannot have dependents under 18 at the time you enlist.

How Many People Are There in the Military and Where Do They Work?

There are 2.2 million people in the armed forces and 5.5 percent are women. Women were first accepted into military academies in 1976. The only jobs closed to women, by an act of Congress, are those in actual combat and those related to combat (flying, says the air force). The rights of women in the military have changed in the last few years. Women now can be married, have dependents, get maternity leave whether married or not, and have equal benefits for themselves and their dependents. The army has 780,000 men and women; the air force 597,000; the navy 565,000; the marines 196,000; and the coast guard 50,000. They are stationed in the United States, mostly in California, Texas, North California, Virginia, Georgia, and Florida; in Europe, mostly in Germany; and in the western Pacific. There are another 3 million men and women in the reserve units.

How Much Money Will I Make?

In 1984, basic pay and allowances for food and quarters for a commissioned officer averaged $33,389 a year. Cash allowances amount to 18 percent of that figure. Also included are medical and dental benefits, 30 days paid vacation, and allowances for living expenses and travel.

What Are the Job Opportunities?

Because the military is now a volunteer rather than a draft organization, it makes its offers as attractive as it can to recruit the number of workers it needs. High unemployment and recession result in many more enlistments. Many young people are interested in military education and training, which will continue to be exceptionally good for learning a skill and getting paid to do so. Peacetime is a good time to find opportunities for work in the military. The more education you have before you join the service, the higher the job level at which you will begin.

Where Can I Get More Information?

Write to or visit your local recruiting station for the latest official information. Look in your phone book, or write to the United States Army Recruiting Command, Fort Sheridan, Illinois 60037. When you are selecting your college, ask about ROTC programs. There are 500 army, navy, marine, and air force ROTC units in colleges.

PEACE CORPS VOLUNTEER

Promotes world peace and friendship by providing trained humanpower to underdeveloped countries, creating a better understanding of Americans and helping Americans to have a better understanding of others

What's It Like To Be a Peace Corps Volunteer?

Judy Daloz, Peace Corps teacher for two years in Nepal, says, "Living alone and working in a foreign culture helped me realize who I am, what I can do, and what I want to do with my life. The experiences I had gave me a perspective on being a woman, on being an American, on being a human being that I doubt I could have gotten otherwise. Although in the beginning I saw it as an exciting challenge to have two years in which to affect people's lives in a positive way, in the end I realized *my* life had been far more affected than those of the people I was living with." Ricardo Campbell, a volunteer in Sao Mateus, Brazil, says there are many reasons for spending two years of your life in the Peace Corps, but a common theme is "the willingness to serve, to step beyond ourselves and our immediate comfort to help, in some small way, other people to help themselves." The daily life of Peace Corps volunteers is on the same economic level and in the same style as the people who have invited them. In Ghana, 105 volunteers are currently involved in raising rabbits and keeping bees for food. They glaze pottery, coke charcoal, and patch dams. They teach speech to retarded children, family planning to medicine men, and plowing with a bullock to farmers who traditionally used only a hoe.

What Education and Skills Will I Need?

High school: Preparation for college. Any skill or professional achievement can be used to be a volunteer in the Peace Corps.

College: Most of the volunteers are liberal arts graduates. The Peace Corps is a temporary work experience, and many volunteers go to graduate school after service. A 13-week training program in the United States is required before leaving the country.

How Many Volunteers Are There and Where Do They Work?

There are only 5,200 volunteers in the Peace Corps, down from 13,000 at its mid-1960s peak. About 40 percent are teachers; 25 percent work in health, nutrition, and water supply; and 18 percent are in food production. Most are college graduates, 20 percent are married and some of these have children. Peace Corps volunteers work in the 60 (formerly 90) countries that have invited them. These places include nations in Africa, Latin America, the Near East, South Asia, and the Pacific areas. Over half of the volunteers are from 23 to 25 years old, 24 percent are from 26 to 28 years old, and 8 percent are over 36 years old. Jane and Gus Root from Vermont joined after they retired from college teaching. Not wanting to do the "expected" consulting, or run a small business, or tend grandchildren, they sold their home and most of their worldly possessions and took off to do volunteer work in the Third World. The Peace Corps attracts, and therefore you will meet, many creative people.

How Much Money Will I Make?

Travel and living allowances are paid. The living allowance is based on the local conditions where the volunteer is working. In Ghana, volunteers earn $270 a month, more than in most other countries because of the high cost of living. Most volunteers accumulate from $1,800 to $2,000 while in the Peace Corps. They usually spend it in traveling for pleasure before returning to the United States after their tour of duty.

What Are the Job Opportunities?

Even though the peak era of the Peace Corps has passed, there will continue to be a need for volunteers of all ages. Peace Corps workers return from overseas with an interest in another area of the world. They have had the opportunity to learn and use a foreign language and to know the culture and traditions of the country in which they worked. Many of the volunteers return home to take advanced work in college. Of those who do not return to school, most enter public service. The following skills are needed and are scarce among applicants: diesel mechanics, foresters, nurses, mathematics and science teachers, and engineers.

Related Careers

Foreign service officer   Missionary
International business

Where Can I Get More Information?

Peace Corps
806 Connecticut Avenue, NW
Washington, D.C. 20525

Call the Peace Corps toll free at 1-800-424-8580, Extension 93.

HEALTH

ABOUT THESE CAREERS

There are 7 million people working in health care, the largest industry in the country. This provides an estimated 400 individual health-care careers, and wide options within each category. The numbers have peaked. Government, insurance companies, and unions are working to cut costs. Hospitals are closing; funds are tight. The trend is to get as many people as possible into outpatient care where costs are less. The jobs go with the patients from hospitals to surgicenters, home health agencies, hospices, and freestanding emergency centers. Doctors are beginning to work for HMOs (health maintenance organizations) taking salaried jobs, while nurses and therapists are doing just the opposite and entering private practice.

Hospitals employ about half of all workers in the health field, although that figure is predicted to be going down. Others work in clinics, home health-care agencies, private practice, laboratories, pharmacies, public health agencies, and mental health centers.

Most of the jobs described here require a number of years of preprofessional and professional college work, and a passing grade on a state licensing examination. Only the jobs of dental hygienist and nurse require less than a four-year program to start in an entry-level position.

Working conditions usually involve long hours. Because health facilities such as nursing homes and hospitals operate around the clock, administrators in these institutions may be called at all hours to settle emergency problems.

There is a major change in the use of computers in the health-care field. No longer used just to manage accounts and medical

179

records, computers are now being used to monitor patients and diagnose diseases. Health is catching up to other industries in the use of computers. The innovations include the use of computers for patient care: to monitor blood pressure, heart rate, temperature, brain pressure; to deliver controlled amounts of heat; to treat tumors in cancer patients; to measure stomach acid; to analyze all the data for determining a patient's condition.

The nursing field employs the largest number of health-care workers—one-third of the total, which represents over 2 million jobs. The demand for nurses will continue to provide an increasing number of jobs, giving nurses more negotiating power as they plan their time and tasks.

The demand for health care will increase as the population grows older and the public becomes increasingly health conscious. Expansion of coverage under prepayment medical programs that make it easier for persons to pay for hospitalization and medical care also contributes to growth in the health group. In addition to jobs created by employment growth, many new jobs will open as a result of turnover and retirement.

Where are there more people than jobs? Besides an oversupply of doctors in private practice in many parts of the country, there is an oversupply of people with a master's in public health and in hospital administration, and there are more general medical technologists than jobs.

And where are the job opportunities? In all areas of nursing; in anesthesiology; in respiratory, occupational, and physical therapy; in home health; in nuclear medicine; and in emergency room medical care.

The late eighties will bring a new focus on the care of the elderly, the applications of sophisticated technology in medical procedures, the prevention of disease, and how to contain costs. There will be more change in the health industry than there has been in its entire history.

ADMINISTRATOR

HEALTH SERVICE ADMINISTRATOR

Plans programs, sets policies, and makes
decisions for hospitals, medical clinics,
nursing homes, HMOs, home health-care
agencies, and other health facilities

What's It Like To Be a Health Service Administrator?

"Health administration takes the same skills that any management career takes, plus the ever-present funding needs of a
nonprofit business," says Elisabeth J. Davis, vice-president of
operations for VNS Homecare, a subsidiary of Visiting Nurse
Service of New York, the biggest nonprofit home health-care
agency in the United States. "What I like most about managing
the VNS is that it fits into my value system. Providing health
care in the home is different because it's in the patient's own
environment—it's easier to get them in on the healing process.
Something special can be worked out, no matter how intense
the care, to make the best possible conditions for the patient.
The difficulties of clerical and paper work are even worse than
those in other fields because we have so many regulatory agencies monitoring everything we do. The challenge of a private
health service is to find the funding for the comprehensive care
we provide our patients, regardless of their income. Medicaid
and Medicare never cover it. We have to get out and do our own
fund-raising, and think of creative ways to cut costs without
cutting services. The VNS has the credible kind of public image
that makes city, state, and national politicians accessible. It
gives me an opportunity to do something political about the
gaps I see in health care. In Vermont, I often meet with United
States Senators Leahy and Stafford to provide them with infor-

mation, to testify, to lobby, and to help write health legislation. I've been in New York City for only a year, but will be meeting with Senator Pat Moynihan soon. I want to start to build my political access in New York, so that once again, my experience in home health-care serves to effect badly needed changes in our nation's health policy."

Edward H. Noroian, executive vice-president of the Presbyterian Hospital of New York City, says, "A hospital is different from other management jobs in that it contains many divisive elements. For the most part, the primary providers of care—the physicians—are not usually employed by the hospital. There are different groups of highly technical employees, a complex physical plant with great energy demands, and a need for fast transfer of information. Furthermore, hospitals are highly regulated. In New York State, more than 160 different regulatory bodies inspect our affairs."

What Education and Skills Will I Need?

High school: Preparation for college, nursing school, or business college.

College: Major in the social sciences, nursing, or business. There are 100 United States colleges and universities that offer degrees in health service administration. Health administrators usually have a master's degree in business or public health, or health administration.

Computer skills: Skill level 4—READ, ENTER, PRINT, SELECT. All managers need the minimum skills to prepare their budgets and reports.

Personal skills: Dealing with millions of dollars worth of facilities and equipment, you will need a command of business and communication skills that allow you to make good decisions and to motivate your employees to implement those decisions. Administrators need to be self-starters. They must enjoy working with people and be able to deal effectively with them. Public speaking is also important.

How Many Health Service Administrators Are There and Where Do They Work?

There are 336,000 administrators; half are women and only 3

percent are black. Most (46 percent) work in hospitals, 19 percent in offices of physicians, and 14 percent in nursing, home health-care, and personal care facilities.

How Much Money Will I Make?

In 1983, administrators with a master's in public health started with an average of $27,000. Hospital administrators are paid according to the size and location of the hospital. The following are averages for 1984: less than 100 beds—$44,000; between 100 and 349 beds—$68,000; between 350 and 1,000 beds—$120,000. Associates ranged from $30,000 to $60,000. Nursing home administrators averaged from $25,000 to $30,000 a year.

What Are the Job Opportunities?

Health facilities are in a crisis because of the increasing needs of the growing number of elderly patients and skyrocketing costs of health care. Hospital care is decreasing, while home health care is increasing. The jobs are competitive because enrollment in public health programs is high, and there are more graduates than jobs.

Related Careers

Business administrator   Social welfare administrator
College administrator

Where Can I Get More Information?

American College of Health Care Executives
840 North Lake Shore Drive
Chicago, Illinois 60611

Association of University Programs in
  Health Administration
1911 Fort Myer Drive, Suite 503
Arlington, Virginia 22209

MEDICAL RECORDS ADMINISTRATOR

Trains and supervises workers who verify, transcribe, code, and maintain files on patients' medical histories; develops systems for documenting, storing, and retrieving medical information

What's It Like To Be a Medical Records Administrator?

Medical records administrators compile statistics and make summaries for reports required by state and health agencies. Medical records include case histories of illnesses, doctors' notes, and X-ray and laboratory reports. Administrators hold meetings with hospital department heads and medical records committees, and plan research projects for the medical team treating the patient.

What Education and Skills Will I Need?

High school: Preparation for college, with emphasis on biological science and computer science.

College: Two or three years of college is usually required before going into one of the 80 approved medical records administration training programs. High school graduates can enter a one-year or two-year college program for medical records technicians. A college degree is required from one of the 85 approved college programs. Programs include anatomy, physiology, hospital administration, and computer science.

Computer skills: Skill level 5—READ, ENTER, PRINT, SELECT, GRAPHICS. Most of the work is on the computer. In addition to the reports, statistics are compiled and analyzed on the computer, and graphics are often required for reports and presentations.

Personal skills: Accuracy, interest in detail, ability to write and speak clearly, and ability to be discreet in handling confidential work are needed by medical records administrators.

How Many Medical Records Administrators Are There and Where Do They Work?

There are 33,000 medical records technicians, mostly women. Most (62 percent) work in hospitals, 13 percent in nursing homes, and 11 percent for the federal government.

How Much Money Will I Make?

In 1984, the average starting salary for registered medical records administrators was $18,000 a year. New graduates started with the federal government at $14,390 a year. Experienced administrators averaged about $24,000 a year, with some earning over $30,000.

What Are the Job Opportunities?

Opportunities will be very good for trained medical records personnel as the number of older people increases and medical records become more complex.

Related Careers

Hospital insurance representative
Medical secretary

Medical librarian

Where Can I Get More Information?

American Medical Records Association
875 North Michigan Avenue, Suite 1850
Chicago, Illinois 60611

PRACTITIONER

CHIROPRACTOR

**Treats patients by manual manipulation of
the body, especially the spinal column**

What's It Like To Be a Chiropractor?

Chiropractic is a system for healing based on the principle that
a person's health is determined by the nervous system. Chiropractors treat their patients by massage, by using water, light,
and heat therapy, and by prescribing diet, exercise, and rest.
They do not use drugs or surgery. Howard Riley, chiropractor
in a small city, sees about 50 patients a week, who range in age
from 6 months to 90 years old. He enjoys the great variety of
people he works with. Dr. Riley doesn't like the necessary insurance forms, the X-ray forms, and the business operations in
general. He advises young people to visit a chiropractor and
observe him or her at work to see what the job is like.

What Education and Skills
Will I Need?

High school: Preparation for college, with as much science as
possible.
College: Two years of college are required for admission to the
15 chiropractic colleges (nine are fully approved by the American Chiropractic Association). The degree of Doctor of Chiropractic (D.C.) is awarded after four years of chiropractic college,
or six years of training after high school.
Computer skills: Skill level 2—READ, ENTER. Everyone in the
medical world must be able to read the terminal and enter patient data.
Personal skills: Manual dexterity, more than strength, is necessary to be a chiropractor, together with sympathetic under-

standing and the skills associated with running a small business.

How Many Chiropractors Are There and Where Do They Work?

There are 31,000 chiropractors and most are men. Ninety-five percent are in private practice and three-fourths practice alone. Half of all chiropractors practice in California, New York, Texas, Missouri, Pennsylvania, and Michigan.

How Much Money Will I Make?

In 1984, experienced chiropractors averaged $60,000 a year.

What Are the Job Opportunities?

The number of graduates is keeping up with the need, giving everyone a job. Much of the demand depends on what kinds of treatment are authorized for payment by medical insurance companies.

Related Careers

Optometrist	Osteopath
Podiatrist	Audiologist

Where Can I Get More Information?

American Chiropractic Association
1916 Wilson Boulevard
Arlington, Virginia 22201

DENTAL HYGIENIST

Cleans teeth, charts tooth conditions,
X-rays teeth, and teaches patients how to
maintain good oral health

What's It Like To Be a Dental Hygienist?

Dental hygienists perform preventive services for patients and teach dental health. Some hygienists work in public school systems promoting health by examining children's teeth and reporting the dental treatment children need to their parents. "I work in a county health department quite independently with my patients in the mornings, and in elementary schools on a dental health program in the afternoons," says Gene F. Sanchez of Michigan, married with two sons. He likes working with educators in the community, and is frustrated by the poor care most people give their teeth and gums. He enjoys the variety of private practice plus working for the public school system.

What Education and Skills Will I Need?

High school: Preparation for a two-year dental program, with emphasis on science. Most dental hygienist university programs require the Dental Aptitude Test for admission. The requirements for admission are usually the same as the requirements for the university's four-year program.

College: Four-year dental hygienist degree programs are available for those who want to go into research or teaching. Each state has its own licensing examination. Most students take a two-year program.

Computer skills: Skill level 2—READ, ENTER. Must be able to read the terminal and enter patient data.

Personal skills: Manual dexterity, ability to help people relax under stress, and neatness are necessary in dental hygiene.

How Many Dental Hygienists Are There and Where Do They Work?

There are 76,000 dental hygienists and 97 percent are women. Most (96 percent) work in dentists' offices. Many are part-time employees.

How Much Money Will I Make?

As in any career dominated by women, salaries are very low. In 1984, the average salary for a two-year dental hygienist was $11 an hour. Beginners working for the federal government made $12,862 to $14,390 a year. In 1985, all hygienists working for the federal government averaged $17,300.

What Are the Job Opportunities?

Opportunities will be good through the 1980s, best in part-time work and rural areas. The oversupply of dentists cuts down on jobs for hygienists, as the dentist will do the hygienist's work when dental work is slow.

Related Careers

Nurse   Medical technologist
Nurse anesthetist   Radiologic technologist

Where Can I Get More Information?

American Dental Hygienists Association
444 North Michigan Avenue
Chicago, Illinois 60611

DENTIST

Examines, diagnoses, and treats various oral diseases and abnormalities

What's It Like To Be a Dentist?

Dentists fill cavities, straighten teeth, take X-rays, treat gums, and perform dental surgery. They clean and examine teeth and mouths as part of preventive dental work. Most of their time is spent with patients, and usually their laboratory work is sent out to dental technicians. Orthodontist Suzanne Rothenberg's mother and father were both dentists. She finds dentistry an exciting career because she can adapt her work to whatever interests her most—patients, research, or teaching. Dentists are independent and can work the hours and days they want. Rothenberg urges young women to major in science so that they can choose dentistry and get in on a high paying job with flexibility for family life.

What Education and Skills Will I Need?

High school: Preparation for a predental program in college, with as much science as possible.

College: Two years of college are required for admission to one of the 20 approved four-year dental schools. Nearly half of the dental schools now require three years of college, and most dental students have a college degree. Predental work includes chemistry, English, biology, and physics.

Computer skills: Skill level 2—READ, ENTER. All health personnel need to be able to read and enter patient data. Many dentists use the computer for billing and medical records as well.

Personal skills: A good visual memory, excellent judgment of space and shape, a delicate touch, and a high degree of manual dexterity are necessary for dentists.

How Many Dentists Are There and Where Do They Work?

There are 156,000 dentists; only 3 percent are women and 2

percent are black. Most (88 percent) work in private offices, others for the federal government and industry.

How Much Money Will I Make?

In 1984, the average income for dentists was $60,000 a year for generalists, and $95,000 for specialists. Dentists started with the federal government at $26,400 a year.

What Are the Job Opportunities?

There is an oversupply of dentists, especially in some parts of the country where dental schools are located. Jobs will continue to be competitive through the 1980s. Dentists are working more evenings and weekends, and using hygienists less, to create more work for themselves.

Related Careers

Optometrist   Physician
Podiatrist

Where Can I Get More Information?

American Dental Association
211 East Chicago Avenue
Chicago, Illinois 60611

DOCTOR

**Diagnoses diseases and treats people who
are ill; also works in research,
rehabilitation, and preventive medicine**

What's It Like To Be a Doctor?

"Very exciting, fatiguing, satisfying. It pays better than most careers. The hours are long, but there is high degree of independence," says Dr. Mary Jane Gray, who combines private practice, research, and teaching at Duke University's Medical Center in North Carolina. Dr. Gray describes her day as follows: "Mornings begin with a lecture or conference, rounds and consultations in the hospital, and laboratory work or operating. Afternoons consist of office hours once a week or research lab four days a week. Evenings include one or two professional meetings a week, a few hours of work at home, and deliveries of babies as they occur."

Resident Julius Boenello says that residents work an average of 100 to 110 hours a week for three to five years. He stresses that young people will need the ambition to put the necessary time into the training. "You really have to give up your personal life for most of this time. If you're married, you never see your family. If you're single, you don't have a chance to be with friends. But the training is all a means to an end. Brighter days are ahead when you practice on your own."

What Education and Skills Will I Need?

High school: Preparation for college by taking as much science and mathematics as offered. A strong B average in the sciences and top motivation for staying in premed and medical school are the main requirements. You don't have to be a genius to go into medicine, as many students are led to believe.

College: Premedicine or biology are the usual majors to prepare for one of the 127 accredited medical colleges. In addition to the physical sciences, the behavioral sciences and computer sciences are becoming more important in medical education. After graduation from a four-year medical school, one year of internship is required to be licensed to practice. Interns are paid by the hospital. The internship is followed by one or more years of residency, depending on what field of medicine the physician is specializing in.

Computer skills: Skill level 2—READ, ENTER. Like all health personnel, you have to be able to read the terminal and enter patient data. For teaching and research more advanced computer skills are needed.

Personal skills: A strong interest and desire to serve the sick and injured are needed, as are persistence for continued study and ability to make fast decisions in emergencies.

How Many Doctors Are There and Where Do They Work?

There are 476,000 doctors; 15 percent are women, and only 2 percent are black. The percentage of black medical students (5.6) is down from 6.3 percent ten years ago. A third of black students are concentrated in three predominantly black medical schools: Howard University in Washington, Morehouse in Atlanta, and Meharry Medical College in Nashville. Most (48 percent) doctors are in private practice, 30 percent are on hospital staffs, and 8 percent work for the federal government. Women make up only 15 percent of all doctors, but there are double that number of women in medical school who will soon be out and practicing.

How Much Money Will I Make?

Doctors are one of the top dozen biggest moneymakers. They averaged $108,400 in 1984; those in pediatrics and family medicine earned a little less, and surgeons averaged $152,000 a year. In 1985, medical school graduates who had completed three years of residency started with the Veterans Administration hospitals at $44,500 a year. In addition, they received up to $13,000 in other cash benefits. Residents made from $20,000 to $24,000 a year and in addition get their room and board in hospital housing.

What Are the Job Opportunities?

There is a surplus of doctors on the market and competition for postgraduate residencies is stiff. Enrollment in medical schools has been going up, and the costs of starting a private practice and paying malpractice insurance has drastically increased.

The best chances for jobs are in inner-city and rural areas and in the fields of public health, medical research, industrial medicine, and rehabilitation.

Related Careers

Dentist   Optometrist
Veterinarian   Audiologist

Where Can I Get More Information?

American Medical Association
Council on Medical Education
535 North Dearborn Street
Chicago, Illinois 60610

NURSE

Observes, assesses, and records symptoms, reactions, and progress of patients; administers medications; helps rehabilitate patients; instructs patients and family members in proper health care; and helps maintain a physical and emotional environment that promotes recovery

What's It Like To Be a Nurse?

Nurses work with patients and families in a variety of settings. They provide direct care to patients in hospitals and nursing homes. They teach patients how to prevent complications and to promote good health practices at home. Within the hospital setting, there are areas of specialization, such as psychiatric nursing, coronary care, intensive care, pediatric nursing, and obstetrics. Nurses who provide direct care to patients are called *staff nurses,* or *primary care nurses.* Administrators who provide indirect care to patients are *head nurses* or *coordinators, team leaders,* and *supervisors.* Nurses also provide care to clients and families in the community. *Public health* and *home health nurses* provide direct care to patients who have been discharged from the hospital, or who do not need hospitalization. They also teach health and health practices, provide immunizations, and work with teachers, parents, and doctors in the community, home, and school. *Office nurses* help physicians care for patients in private practices or clinics. *Private duty nurses* work in patients' homes or in hospitals to take care of one patient who needs special and constant attention. After advanced training, *nurse practitioners* provide primary health care as independent decision makers. They often establish a joint practice with a physician or run their own clinics. "You seldom see a male nurse on television," says Kenneth Zwolski, a former science teacher who is enrolled in nursing school. "Now that I'm right where the action is, I'm amazed at what's available in terms of future career opportunities. I can do a great variety of jobs as a nurse."

What Education and Skills Will I Need?

High school: Preparation for nursing education, with a college preparatory program and an emphasis on science.

College: A bachelor's degree is required to become a professional nurse; all others are considered technical nurses. There are, however, three types of registered nurse (RN) education: a three-year diploma program conducted by a hospital, a bachelor's degree in a college, or an associate degree program offered in a two-year junior or community college. Nurses who plan a career in teaching and research will be required to get a doctorate in nursing. There are many opportunities for specialization through a master's degree program, including a master's in public health administration.

Computer skills: Skill level 2—READ, ENTER. Nurses must be able to read the terminal and enter patient data.

Personal skills: Ability to accept responsibility, initiative, good judgment, good mental and physical stamina, and an ability to make reasoned decisions.

How Many Nurses Are There and Where Do They Work?

There are 1,312,000 registered nurses; 96 percent are women, 8 percent are black. Most (66 percent) work in hospitals. Others are employed by agencies, nursing homes, the government, or families for private duty.

How Much Money Will I Make?

In 1984, the median income for all nurses was $21,000 a year, the top 10 percent making more than $31,000. Nursing home nurses make less; the median was $17,300 a year. Hospital nurses started at an average of $18,800, and experienced hospital nurses averaged $25,300. Nurse anesthetists averaged $37,300 a year. The Veteran's Administration paid nurses with a bachelor's degree $18,763 to start and experienced nurses $24,500.

What Are the Job Opportunities?

Excellent through the 1980s. Nursing may be one of the most exciting, expansive, developing professions in the next decade. Salaries, advancement, and fringe benefits are increasing rapidly. There is a shortage of nurses, providing a diversity of opportunities. Increasing numbers of men are entering nursing as they learn that the 1.5 percent unemployment rate for nurses is one of the lowest in the entire work force.

Related Careers

Occupational therapist   Physical therapist
Physician's assistant

Where Can I Get More Information?

American Nurses' Association
2420 Pershing Road
Kansas City, Missouri 64108

National League for Nursing
10 Columbus Circle
New York, New York 10019

OPTOMETRIST

**Examines people's eyes for vision problems
and disease, and tests eyes for depth, color,
and focus perceptions**

What's It Like To Be an Optometrist?

"I work with contact lenses. They change the client's looks completely. When a client is happy with the results, it makes my day," says optometrist Geno Grattini, father of three preschool children. "I work from 8 a.m. until 6 p.m. and I like every aspect of my work. I'm my own boss and I make all decisions. The most exciting part of the work is when I hold up different lenses for children and ask them what they can see, and they give me a 'cat who ate the canary' grin, suddenly realizing the things they haven't seen clearly before."

What Education and Skills Will I Need?

High school: Preparation for college, with an emphasis on science.

College: Two years of college are required for admission to the four-year program of the College of Optometry to become a Doctor of Optometry (O.D.). Subjects required in college are English, mathematics, biology, physics, and chemistry. There are 13 accredited schools of optometry in the United States.

Computer skills: Skill level 2—READ, ENTER. Reading the terminal and entering client data are usually necessary. Many optometrists do their billing by computer as well.

Personal skills: Business ability (most optometrists are self-employed), self-discipline, and tact with patients are needed.

How Many Optometrists Are There and Where Do They Work?

There are 29,000 optometrists and only three percent are women. Seventy percent work in their own offices and others work for retail optical goods stores.

How Much Money Will I Make?

In 1984, beginning optometrists averaged $27,000 a year. Experienced optometrists averaged $55,000 a year.

What Are the Job Opportunities?

The increasing older population and health insurance coverage of vision problems will continue to contribute to good job opportunities.

Related Careers

Chiropractor   Podiatrist
Dentist

Where Can I Get More Information?

American Optometric Association
243 Lindbergh Boulevard
St. Louis, Missouri 63141

OSTEOPATHIC PHYSICIAN

Diagnoses and treats diseases with special emphasis on the musculoskeletal system— bones, muscles, ligaments, and nerves

What's It Like To Be an Osteopathic Physician?

One of the basic treatments used by osteopathic physicians centers on manipulating the musculoskeletal system with the hands. Doctors of osteopathy also use surgery, drugs, and all other accepted methods of medical care. Most osteopathic physicians are in family practice and engage in general medicine. These physicians usually see patients in their offices, make house calls, and treat patients in one of the 200 osteopathic hospitals.

What Education and Skills Will I Need?

High school: Preparation for college, with science and mathematics courses.

College: Most osteopathic students have college degrees, with courses that include biology, chemistry, physics, and English to qualify for a three- or four-year program in one of the 13 schools of osteopathy where they are awarded the degree of Doctor of Osteopathy (D.O.).

Computer skills: Skill level 2—READ, ENTER. All doctors must be able to read the terminal and enter patient data.

Personal skills: A strong interest in osteopathic principles of healing, a keen sense of touch, and self-confidence are needed.

How Many Osteopathic Physicians Are There and Where Do They Work?

There are 20,000 D.O.s and 87 percent are men. Almost 85 percent are in private practice, chiefly in states with osteopathic hospitals. Three-fifths of all osteopathic physicians practice in Florida, Michigan, Pennsylvania, New Jersey, Ohio, Texas, Missouri, and Washington, D.C. More than half practice in towns with fewer than 50,000 people.

How Much Money Will I Make?

In 1984, the average for family physicians, including osteopathic physicians, was $71,000 a year.

What Are the Job Opportunities?

Chances for work will be very good though the 1980s, especially in states with osteopathic hospitals.

Related Careers

Chiropractor   Optometrist
Dentist

Where Can I Get More Information?

American Association of Colleges of Osteopathic Medicine
6110 Executive Boulevard
Rockville, Maryland 20852

PODIATRIST

Prevents, diagnoses, and treats foot diseases and injuries

What's It Like To Be a Podiatrist?

Podiatrists take X-rays and perform pathological tests to diagnose foot diseases. Depending on the condition, they perform surgery, fit corrective devices and proper shoes, and prescribe drugs and physical therapy. They treat corns, bunions, calluses, ingrown toe nails, skin and nail diseases, deformed toes, and arch disabilities. Most podiatrists are generalists and provide all types of foot care.

What Education and Skills Will I Need?

High school: Preparation for college, with strong science and mathematics.
Colleges: Most podiatric medicine students are college graduates and go on to one of the six podiatric schools for four years.
Computer skills: Skill level 2—READ, ENTER. Reading the terminal and entering patient data are usually required. Many podiatrists use the computer for billing and running their business.
Personal skills: Manual dexterity, scientific interest, ability for detailed work, and a pleasant personality are all helpful for success in podiatry.

How Many Podiatrists Are There and Where Do They Work?

There are 13,000 podiatrists and about 5 percent are women. Fifty-five percent work in their own business, 16 percent in hospitals, and 10 percent in nursing homes.

How Much Money Will I Make?

In 1984, podiatrists averaged from $26,381 to $31,619 a year. Established podiatrists made over $50,000 a year.

What Are the Job Opportunities?

The opportunities are very good because of growing population of older patients and because podiatry is well covered by health insurance.

Related Careers

Chiropractor   Dentist
Optometrist

Where Can I Get More Information?

American Association of Colleges of Podiatric Medicine
6110 Executive Boulevard, Suite 204
Rockville, Maryland 20852

VETERINARIAN

**Prevents, diagnoses, treats, and controls
diseases and injuries of animals**

What's It Like To Be a Veterinarian?

Veterinarians treat animals in hospitals and clinics or on farms or ranches. They perform surgery on sick and injured animals and prescribe and administer drugs, medicines, and vaccines. A large number of vets specialize in the health and breeding of cattle, poultry, sheep, swine, or horses. Their work is important for the nation's food production and also for public health. Amy Merrit, D.V.M. (Doctor of Veterinary Medicine), is a partner in a Kansas clinic. She likes the physical and intellectual challenge of her career. She says a vet must really have an inquiring mind. "So much of veterinary medicine is a puzzle, and there is no book of treatments to cover all diseases or solve most of the problems." Specialties in veterinary medicine include research medicine, federal health services, teaching, hospital staff, self-employment, or working in a partnership or clinic.

What Education and Skills Will I Need?

High school: Preparation for college, with emphasis on biological sciences.
College: Two years of preveterinary medicine is required for admission into one of the 27 accredited four-year veterinary colleges.
Computer skills: Skill level 2—READ, ENTER. Reading the terminal and entering medical records are necessary. Many use computers for billing as well.
Personal skills: Ability to communicate with animals is important, as is interest in food, health, and science. Since many animals are outside, a love of the outdoors is helpful.

How Many Veterinarians Are There and Where Do They Work?

There are 40,000 veterinarians and only 3 percent are women. Most (66 percent) work for agricultural services, 15 percent work for the federal government, and the remainder are in private practice.

How Much Money Will I Make?

In 1984, veterinarians made an average of $46,000 a year in private practice. The federal government started vets at $24,700, and paid experienced vets an average of $40,000 a year.

What Are the Job Opportunities?

The best opportunities are for those who specialize in small-animal practice, toxicology, and pathology. Jobs with veterinary firms are competitive because the number of graduates has greatly increased.

Related Careers

Dentist	Doctor
Chiropractor	Podiatrist

Where Can I Get More Information?

American Veterinary Medical Association
390 North Meacham Road
Schaumburg, Illinois 60196

THERAPIST

OCCUPATIONAL THERAPIST

**Plans and directs activities to help patients
return to work, and generally helps
patients adjust to their disability**

What's It Like To Be an Occupational Therapist?

The occupational therapist works as a member of a medical team with a doctor, physical therapist, vocational counselor, nurse, and social worker. They teach manual and creative skills such as weaving, clay modeling, leather working, and commercial skills that may increase motor skills, strength, and motivation. The goals of the therapist are to help patients to gain stability, combat boredom during long illnesses, and develop independence in routine daily activities such as eating, dressing, and writing.

What Education and Skills Will I Need?

High school: Preparation for college, with emphasis on science, crafts, and social science.
College: Sixty-three colleges and universities offer degrees in occupational therapy. Many college graduates go into occupa-

tional therapy after college from a variety of majors—often biology or physical education—and get a master's degree in occupational therapy in one year.

Computer skills: Skill level 2—READ, ENTER. Health personnel need to be able to read the terminal and enter patient data.

Personal skills: A supportive attitude toward the sick and disabled, manual skills, maturity, patience, and imagination are needed.

How Many Occupational Therapists Are There and Where Do They Work?

There are 25,000 occupational therapists and 90 percent are women. Most (43 percent) work in hospitals, 17 percent work in educational services, and 11 percent work for state and local government.

How Much Money Will I Make?

In 1984, the average salaries were from $21,300 to $25,700 a year. Directors earned more than $33,000 a year, and beginners with the federal government started at $18,900 a year.

What Are the Job Opportunities?

The future is expected to be excellent through the 1980s with over 2,000 new job openings each year until 1995. Occupational therapy is one of the top 20 fastest growing occupations. The increasing older population, survival of children with birth defects, and lower enrollments in occupational therapy programs will result in more jobs than graduates.

Related Careers

Physical therapist   Speech therapist
Rehabilitation counselor   Recreation worker

Where Can I Get More Information?

American Occupational Therapy Association
1383 Piccard Drive
Rockville, Maryland 20852

PHYSICAL THERAPIST

Uses exercise, massage, heat, water, and electricity to treat and rehabilitate people with disabilities

What's It Like To Be a Physical Therapist?

Physical therapists perform and interpret tests and measurements for muscle strength, motor development, functioning capacity, and respiratory and circulatory efficiency. They plan a program of therapy to include exercises for increasing strength, endurance, and coordination; stimuli to make motor activity and learning easier; instructions to carry out everyday activity; and applications of massage, heat and cold, light, water or electricity to relieve pain or improve the condition of muscles. Ernie Natlette says what interests him most about being a physical therapist is the great variety of patients he deals with—accident victims, crippled children, disabled older persons, cardiac rehabilitation patients, and more. He also likes the interaction with other health-care people working together to help the patients.

What Education and Skills Will I Need?

High school: Preparation for college, with emphasis on science.
College: Most students major in physical therapy in college. A one-year course is offered for college graduates, usually in connection with a hospital program. Many physical education majors and science majors go into this program. There are 89 bachelor's degree programs, 6 certificate programs, and 13 master's degree programs.
Computer skills: Skill level 2—READ, ENTER. Health personnel must be able to read the terminal and enter patient data.
Personal skills: Resourcefulness, patience, manual dexterity, physical stamina, and an ability to work with disabled people and their families are needed to be good in physical therapy.

How Many Physical Therapists Are There and Where Do They Work?

One-fourth of the 58,000 therapists are men. About half work in hospitals, and 16 percent work in offices of physical therapists. The government and the armed forces also employ many physical therapists.

How Much Money Will I Make?

In 1984, beginning physical therapists averaged $19,600 a year. Experienced therapists working for the federal government averaged $24,600, and supervisors made an average of $35,000.

What Are the Job Opportunities?

The opportunities will remain excellent through the 1980s. New graduates are not keeping up with the number of jobs available. Physical therapy is one of the top 20 fastest growing careers.

Related Careers

Occupational therapist   Prosthetist
Speech therapist   Nurse

Where Can I Get More Information?

American Physical Therapy Association
1111 North Fairfax Street
Alexandria, Virginia 22314

SPEECH AND HEARING THERAPIST

Diagnoses and treats people who cannot speak or hear clearly

What's It Like To Be a Speech and Hearing Therapist?

A speech and hearing therapist, sometimes called a speech pathologist and audiologist, works with children or adults who have communication disorders (speech, hearing, language, learning). This work may be with one person or with small groups. Lessons vary from one-half hour to group classes of two hours and deal with such problems as stuttering and defective articulation, as well as various speech and hearing impediments caused by brain damage, mental retardation, or emotional disturbance. The responsibility of the therapist is to identify and evaluate the disorder; consult with the other specialists involved, such as the physician, psychologist, social worker, or counselor; and organize a program of therapy.

What Education and Skills Will I Need?

High school: Preparation for college, with a strong science program.

College: Most students major in speech pathology and audiology, or in any related field such as education, psychology, or education for the blind or deaf, to prepare for graduate school. A master's degree from one of the 245 college programs is required for professional certification in most states. Many scholarships and fellowships are available from graduate schools through the United States Vocational Rehabilitation Administration.

Computer skills: Skill level 2—READ, ENTER. Health personnel need to know how to read the terminal and enter patient data.

Personal skills: Patience with slow progress, responsibility, objectivity, ability to work with detail, and concern for the needs of others are important for therapists.

How Many Speech and Hearing Therapists Are There and Where Do They Work?

One-fourth of the 47,000 speech and hearing therapists are men. Most of them (91 percent) work in hospital programs.

How Much Money Will I Make?

In 1984, the average salary range in hospitals and medical centers was from $19,800 to $34,900 a year. Speech pathologists started a little higher than audio therapists.

What Are the Job Opportunities?

Job opportunities will be very good through the 1980s. Increased numbers of young school children will result in new jobs for graduates.

Related Careers

Occupational therapist   Physical therapist
Teacher   Optometrist

Where Can I Get More Information?

American Speech–Language–Hearing Association
10801 Rockville Pike
Bethesda, Maryland 20852

OTHER HEALTH CAREERS

DIETITIAN

**Plans nutritious meals to help people
maintain or recover good health**

What's It Like To Be a Dietitian?

Administrative dietitians apply the principles of nutrition and management to large-scale meal planning and preparation, such as that done in hospitals, prisons, company cafeterias, and schools. Hospital dietitians plan modified meals, teach special diets to hospital patients and outpatients, and consult with doctors and nurses concerning the special needs of patients who must also take prescribed drugs. The primary responsibility of the dietitian is to teach other professionals in the hospital the value of nutrition for patients trying to recover good health. Because a hospital functions 24 hours a day, 365 days a year, a dietitian's schedule includes all hours and all days.

What Education and Skills Will I Need?

High school: Preparation for college, with an emphasis on sciences.

College: Preparation for a degree in foods and nutrition or in institutional management. To qualify for professional recognition, take one of the 67 approved one-year internships in a hospital. Most of the top jobs are offered to students who have completed an internship, which provides further education and on-the-job experience under supervision.

Computer skills: Skill level 5—READ, ENTER, PRINT, SELECT, GRAPHICS. Dietitians often plan their programs on the computer, and use graphics to present their plans and educational programs to other professional personnel.

Personal skills: An aptitude for science and organizational and administrative abilities are needed as well as the ability to work well with other people.

How Many Dietitians Are There and Where Do They Work?

There are 48,000 dietitians and 10 percent are men. Most (38 percent) work in hospitals, 17 percent in nursing homes, 14 percent for social service agencies, and 7 percent for local government.

How Much Money Will I Make?

In 1984, beginning salaries for new graduates of an internship program averaged $18,900 a year. Experienced dietitians in hospitals made an average of $28,000 a year.

What Are the Job Opportunities?

Job opportunities will be very good through the 1980s. Industry is offering high salaries and taking a lot of dietitians away from health jobs, causing a shortage in the health fields.

Related Careers

Food technologist   Home economist
Food service manager

Where Can I Get More Information?

The American Dietetic Association
430 North Michigan Avenue
Chicago, Illinois 60611

MEDICAL TECHNOLOGIST

Performs chemical, microscopic,
and bacteriological tests under the
supervision of a pathologist to
diagnose the causes and nature of
diseases

What's It Like To Be a Medical Technologist?

Medical technologists perform blood counts, blood-cholesterol levels, and skin tests. They also examine other body fluids and tissues microscopically for bacteria, fungi, and other organisms. In small hospitals, the medical technologists do all of the tests; in larger hospitals, they specialize in areas such as the study of blood cells or tissue preparation and examination. Medical technologists are usually assisted by medical technicians and laboratory assistants who perform simple, routine tests. Because of the computer revolution, the tasks of medical technologists are rapidly changing as routine tests are performed by computer. Now more specialization is required of the technologist.

What Education and Skills Will I Need?

High school: Preparation for college, with emphasis on science and mathematics.
College: A college degree program or one year of special training after three years of college is required. Chemistry, biology, mathematics, and computer science are required courses.
Computer skills: Skill level 4—READ, ENTER, PRINT, SELECT. Technologists spend a lot of time on the computer, usually with programs that are highly specialized, and which they learn on the job.
Personal skills: Manual dexterity and good eyesight are essential, as well as accuracy, dependability, and the ability to work under pressure.

How Many Medical Technologists Are There and Where Do They Work?

There are 236,000 medical technicians and technologists. About 50,000 are technologists; 10,000 are men and 5,000 are black. Most (70 percent) work in hospitals, 12 percent in doctors' offices, and 11 percent for medical and dental laboratories.

How Much Money Will I Make?

In 1980, the average starting salary was $18,200 a year. Experienced technologists averaged $23,700 a year. Chief technologists made from $25,000 to $31,000.

What Are the Job Opportunities?

Chances for a job will be very good through the 1980s. Increased use of laboratory tests for chemotherapy patients, for example, creates more jobs. The demands are for those with advanced technological skills, because computer systems will increasingly do the routine work.

Related Careers

Chemistry technologist   Criminologist
Food tester

Where Can I Get More Information?

American Medical Technologists
710 Higgins Road
Park Ridge, Illinois 60068

PHARMACIST

**Selects, compounds, dispenses, and
preserves drugs and medicines to fill the
prescriptions of physicians
and dentists**

What's It Like To Be a Pharmacist?

"I dispense medication to hospital patients and staff, write up orders to pharmaceutical houses, compound and manufacture pharmaceuticals, and give drug information over the telephone to questioning nurses and physicians," says June Marie Jones, assistant director of pharmacy in a university hospital. "In addition, I meet with nursing staff to discuss patient care and pharmacy, meet with physicians, and write the *Pharmacy Bulletin,* which informs doctors and nurses about the latest drug information. After gaining experience, I plan to go into business for myself. Most women in pharmacy work for others. I've decided I want to be the owner of a drugstore—where the money is."

What Education and Skills Will I Need?

High school: Preparation for college, with biology, chemistry, and computer science.

College: Pharmacy is a five-year college program leading to a degree. Such programs are offered by 72 accredited colleges and universities in the United States. The program includes chemistry, physics, mathematics, computer science, zoology, and physiology. Each state requires that pharmacists have their own licenses to practice.

Computer skills: Skill level 3—READ, ENTER, PRINT. Most pharmacists have a specialized program and need only minimum skills, learned on the job.

Personal skills: Business ability, an interest in medicine, orderliness, accuracy, and the ability to build customers' confidence are needed for success in pharmacy.

How Many Pharmacists Are There and Where Do They Work?

There are 151,000 pharmacists; 24 percent are women and 4 percent are black. Most work in drug stores (65 percent) and hospitals (25 percent).

How Much Money Will I Make?

Pharmacy pays better than most health-related careers that require the same level of education. In 1984, beginning pharmacists earned $24,700 a year with the federal government. In hospitals experienced pharmacists earned a median of $29,600, with the top 10 percent making more than $41,900 a year. Independent pharmacists averaged $28,200 a year, and many made much more than that if they owned the store.

What Are the Job Opportunities?

Jobs in urban areas will be competitive because there is an oversupply of pharmacists in major cities. Elsewhere, the chances for a job will be very good through the 1980s. The increasing age of the population and health insurance coverage of prescription drugs will expand the need for pharmacists.

Related Careers

Pharmaceutical chemist
Dietitian

Pharmaceutical sales representative

Where Can I Get More Information?

American Pharmaceutical Association
2215 Constitution Avenue, NW
Washington, D.C. 20037

SCIENCE AND TECHNOLOGY

ABOUT THESE CAREERS

More than three million people, or nearly one-quarter of all professional workers, are engineers, scientists, or other scientific and technical workers. The number of engineers has tripled in the past 30 years. Careers for more than two million jobs are described in this cluster.

A bachelor's degree is usually needed to enter scientific and engineering jobs. In mathematics and physical and biological sciences, more emphasis is placed on advanced degrees. For some careers, such as astronomer, a doctorate is required for full professional status. Undergraduate training for scientists and engineers includes courses in their major field and in related science areas, including mathematics. Courses and skills in computer science are important for all engineers and scientists.

Students who want to specialize in a particular area of science should select their schools carefully. For example, those who plan to become biomedical engineers or biochemists and work in medicine should study at a university affiliated with a research hospital. Those who want to be agricultural scientists can get the most practical training at universities with agricultural research and development programs.

Working conditions in scientific and technical careers, such as forester, range manager, engineer, geologist, and meteorologist, can involve considerable time away from home working outdoors in remote parts of the country. Foresters may also work extra hours on emergency duty, such as in firefighting or on search-and-rescue missions. Many engineers spend some time in factories or mines, at construction sites, or at other outdoor locations. Others work under quiet conditions in modern offices and research laboratories. Exploration geologists often work overseas. They travel to remote sites by helicopter and jeep, and cover large areas by foot, often working in teams. Geologists in mining sometimes work underground. Meteorologists in small weather stations generally work alone; those in large stations work as part of a team.

New engineering graduates begin working under the close supervision of experienced engineers. To determine the specialties for which graduates are best suited, many companies have programs to acquaint new engineers with industrial practices. Experienced engineers may advance to positions of greater responsibility; those with proven ability often become managers, and increasingly large numbers are being promoted to top management jobs. Some engineers get an MBA degree to improve their advancement opportunities, while others go after law degrees and become patent attorneys or consultants.

Science and technology are the fields with the most jobs. These are the computer-age jobs. If you want to have the best job opportunities, think seriously about science and technology. Whatever your career choice, add some technical skills to your credentials so that you can translate the arts, business, or social sciences into computer-age career opportunities.

AGRICULTURAL SCIENTIST

Studies farm crops and animals and develops ways of improving quantity and quality

What's It Like To Be an Agricultural Scientist?

Agricultural scientists apply biological science to solving practical problems in agriculture. They usually specialize as one of the following: *Agronomists* are concerned with the growth and improvement of field crops. They develop new growth methods and ways to control disease, pests, and weeds. *Animal scientists* do research on the breeding, feeding, and diseases of farm animals. *Horticulturists* work with orchard and garden plants such as fruit and nut trees, vegetables, and flowers. Besides food, they seek to improve plant cultivation methods for the beautification of communities, homes, and parks. *Soil scientists* study soil characteristics, map soil types, and determine the best types of crops for each soil.

What Education and Skills Will I Need?

High school: Preparation for college with an emphasis on science.

College: Each state has at least one land-grant college that offers agricultural science. Many students major in biology, chemistry, or physics, and get a graduate degree in agriculture.

Computer skills: Skill level 4—READ, ENTER, PRINT, SELECT. Computer proficiency is required for all research and most practical jobs.

Personal skills: Ability to work independently or as part of a team, and the ability to communicate findings clearly and concisely, both orally and in writing.

How Many Agricultural Scientists Are There and Where Do They Work?

There are 20,000 agricultural scientists; most of them are men. Many work for universities (21 percent), others work for local government (16 percent), the federal government (14 percent), and still others for agricultural businesses and services (11 percent).

How Much Money Will I Make?

In 1984, the average starting salary for someone with a bachelor's degree was $17,000. The federal government started agricultural scientists with a master's degree at $17,824 to $21,804, and paid experienced agricultural scientists an average of $33,600.

What Are the Job Opportunities?

Jobs are expected to be scarce through the mid-1990s because government jobs are down. Best bets are with agriculture-related businesses.

Related Careers

Chemist   Extension service
Conservationist   Horticulturist

Where Can I Get More Information?

American Society of Agronomy
677 South Segoe Road
Madison, Wisconsin 53711

BIOLOGIST

**Studies the structure, evolution, behavior,
and life processes of living organisms**

What's It Like To Be a Biologist?

Major industry is just beginning to find applications for the new biology, that is, genetic engineering to manufacture living materials. For example, bacteria are being used to convert sunlight into electrochemical energy. More traditional biologists are working to improve medicine, to increase crop yields, and to improve our natural environment. Biological scientists include many specialists, such as botanists who study all aspects of plant life, and zoologists who study animal life and usually specialize in birds, insects, or mammals. The bigger fields of biological specialization are genetics, horticulture, nutrition, and pharmacology. Biological scientists usually work in the field or in a laboratory with a team of scientists, publish their findings, and also teach. Sometimes called life scientists, they study all aspects of living organisms, emphasizing the relationship of animals and plants to their environment. Creating entirely new foods and fibers by cheap and simple methods will be major challenges to biologists of the eighties.

What Education and Skills Will I Need?

High school: Preparation for college and graduate school, with as much science, mathematics, and computer science as offered in high school.

College: Major in any biological science and get as broad an understanding as possible of all sciences, including chemistry, physics, and computer science.

Computer skills: Skill level 4—READ, ENTER, PRINT, SELECT. All scientists need this level of proficiency.

Personal skills: Independent working skills, ability to work with a team, curiosity, and good communication skills are necessary for the biologist.

How Many Biologists Are There and Where Do They Work?

There are 52,000 biologists; 46 percent are women and 5 percent are black. Many of them (26 percent) work for the federal government; others work for state government (14 percent), for chemical manufacturers (12 percent), and for research and development businesses (11 percent).

How Much Money Will I Make?

In 1984, private industry offered an average of $16,800 a year for biologists with a bachelor's degree. Biologists with master's degrees began at $17,824 to $21,804 a year with the federal government. Average salaries for all biologists in the federal government were $35,500 a year.

What Are the Job Opportunities?

Jobs are expected to be excellent through the mid-1990s, especially in private industry, in research, and in areas related to the genetic, cellular, and biochemical areas of biology. Advanced degrees will be required.

Related Careers

Forester

Biochemist

Soil conservationist

Agricultural scientist

Where Can I Get More Information?

American Institute of Biological Sciences

1401 Wilson Boulevard

Arlington, Virginia 22209

CHEMIST

Studies the properties and composition of
matter; often performs chemical tests on
manufactured goods such as drugs,
plastics, dyes, paint, and petroleum
products

What's It Like To Be a Chemist?

In basic research, a chemist investigates ways to create or improve new products. The process of developing a product begins with descriptions of the characteristics it should have. If similar products exist, chemists test samples to determine their ingredients. If no such product exists, they experiment with various substances until they develop a product with the required specifications. Their research has resulted in the development of a tremendous variety of synthetic materials. Chemists usually specialize to become one of the following: an *analytical chemist* who determines the composition and nature of substances; an *organic chemist* who studies the chemistry of living things; an *inorganic chemist* who studies compounds other than carbon; a *physical chemist* who studies energy; or a *biochemist* who studies life science. Some biochemists go into biotechnology and become *genetic engineers.* There are now over 5,000 of these engineers, who design or alter the genetic material of animals and plants to enable them to do things they cannot do naturally.

In medicine, biotechnology will lead to new, better, and cheaper drugs.

What Education and Skills Will I Need?

High school: Preparation for college, with as much science, mathematics, and computer science as possible.

College: Over 1,100 colleges offer a bachelor's degree in chemistry. Mathematics and physics are required for all chemists. The top jobs in research require a Ph.D. with computer skills.

Computer skills: Skill level 4—READ, ENTER, PRINT, SELECT. This level is required for all science careers.

Personal skills: Interest in studying mathematics and science, good hand coordination for building scientific apparatus, and ability to concentrate on detail are essential to the chemist.

How Many Chemists Are There and Where Do They Work?

There are 89,000 chemists; 20 percent are women and 5 percent are black. Chemists work for chemical product manufacturers (37 percent), research and development labs (11 percent), durable goods manufacturers (10 percent), and the federal government (10 percent).

How Much Money Will I Make?

In 1984, private industry started college graduates at $21,100, master's degree graduates at $26,700, and Ph.D.s at $35,500 a year. Experienced chemists with Ph.D.s averaged $49,000 a year.

What Are the Job Opportunities?

Most jobs will be in private industry, especially in the area of development of new products. Biochemists with advanced degrees will have the best job opportunities.

Related Careers

Agricultural scientist   Biological scientist
Chemical engineer   Physicist

Where Can I Get More Information?

American Chemical Society
1155 16th Street, NW
Washington, D.C. 20036

CONSERVATIONIST

**Manages, develops, and protects forests,
rangelands, wildlife, soil, and water
resources**

What's It Like To Be a Conservationist?

Foresters often specialize in timber management, outdoor recreation, or forest economics. They deal with one of our most important natural resources, trees, which must be protected from fire, harmful insects, and disease. Foresters plan and supervise the growing, protection, and harvesting of trees. Range managers, sometimes called range conservationists, range scientists, or range ecologists, determine the number and kind of animals to be grazed, the grazing system to be used, and the best grazing season for yielding a high livestock production. At the same time, they must conserve soil and vegetation for other uses, such as wildlife grazing, outdoor recreation, and timber production. Soil conservationists help farmers and ranchers with conservation of soil and water. They prepare maps with the soil, water, and vegetation plans of the farmer's land, recommend ways land can best be used, and help estimate costs and returns on land use. Chip Williams, graduate student in forestry economics, has enjoyed his college studies since committing himself to a specific career. He says, "Now all of my coursework has a purpose and falls into place. What excites me about forestry is the scientific knowledge. I thought it was a little more 'woodsy' than it is. I spend most of my study hours figuring out things related to forestry."

What Education and Skills Will I Need?

High school: Preparation for college with as much science as possible.

College: Major in one of the 46 approved forestry programs or in range science, which is offered at 20 universities.

Computer skills: Skill level 2—PRINT, ENTER. The minimum level necessary for all careers; research requires more.

Personal skills: A love of the outdoors, physical hardiness, and a scientific curiosity to solve problems is needed to be happy in conservation.

How Many Conservationists Are There and Where Do They Work?

There are 31,000 conservationists and foresters; 7 percent are women and 3 percent are black. Conservationists work for the federal government (46 percent), for state government (20 percent), and in the forestry industry (15 percent).

How Much Money Will I Make?

Beginning foresters in private industry averaged $14,400 a year in 1984. The average salary for all foresters was $31,000. A range conservationist made $26,600 with the federal government and a soil conservationist made $28,100.

What Are the Job Opportunities?

Government budget cuts are resulting in a decreased number of jobs in conservation and forestry. Private industry is the best bet.

Related Careers

Agricultural scientist   Agricultural engineer
Wildlife manager   Biologist

Where Can I Get More Information?

American Forestry Association
1319 18th Street, NW
Washington, D.C. 20036

ENGINEER

Converts raw materials and power into
useful products at a reasonable cost in time
and money

What's It Like To Be an Engineer?

Engineers develop electric power, water supply, and waste disposal systems to meet the problems of urban living. They design machines, artificial organs, and industrial machinery and equipment used to manufacture heating, air-conditioning, and ventilation equipment. Engineers also develop scientific equipment to probe outer space and the ocean depths. They design, plan, and supervise the construction of buildings, highways, and transit systems. They design and develop consumer products such as cars, television sets, video games, and systems for control and automation of business and manufacturing processes.

Most engineers study in one of the more than 25 specialties. Within the basic specialities there are over 85 subdivisions. For example, structural, environmental, hydraulic, and highway engineering are subdivisions of civil engineering. Engineers within each of the branches may apply their specialized knowledge to many fields. For instance, electrical engineers work in medicine, computers, missile guidance, and electric power distribution. Since knowledge of basic engineering principles is required for all areas of engineering, it is possible for engineers to shift from one branch or field of specialization to another, especially during the early stages of their careers.

There are six broad engineering specialities. *Aerospace engineers* (68,000) work on all types of aircraft and spacecraft, including missiles, rockets, and military and commercial planes. They develop aerospace products, from initial planning and design to final assembly and testing. *Chemical engineers* (55,000) design equipment and chemical plants, and determine methods of manufacturing products. Often, they design and operate pilot plans to test their work, and develop chemical processes such as those for removing chemical contaminants from waste materials. *Civil engineers* (165,000) design and supervise the construction of roads, harbors, airports, tunnels, bridges, water supply systems, sewage systems, and buildings. *Electrical en-*

gineers (325,000) design, develop, and supervise the manufacture of electrical and electronic equipment, including electric motors, generators, communications equipment, pacemakers, pollution-measuring instrumentation, radar, computers, lasers, missile guidance systems, and electrical appliances of all kinds. *Industrial engineers* (115,000) design systems for data processing and apply operations-research techniques to organizational, production, and related problems. They also develop management control systems to aid in financial planning and cost analysis; they design production planning and control systems, and design or improve systems to distribute goods and services. *Mechanical engineers* (213,000) design and develop machines that produce power, such as internal combustion engines and nuclear reactors. They also design and develop a great variety of machines that use power, such as refrigeration and air-conditioning equipment, elevators, machine tools, and printing presses. Other engineering specialties include agricultural engineers (12,000), biomedical engineers, (3,000 and growing), ceramic engineers (12,000), metallurgical engineers (17,000), mining engineers (6,000 and growing), and petroleum engineers (20,000).

What Education and Skills Will I Need?

High school: Preparation for college, with an emphasis on science, mathematics, and computer science.
College: Major in engineering at one of the 260 approved colleges.
Computer skills: Skill level 5—READ, ENTER, PRINT, SELECT, GRAPHICS. Engineers use computers as designing tools and must have top skills.
Personal skills: Ability to think analytically, capacity for detail, and ability to work as a team member are necessary skills.

How Many Engineers Are There and Where Do They Work?

There are 1,204,000 engineers; only 5 percent are women and 2 percent are black. Over half of the engineers are employed by manufacturing industries; one-fourth are in construction, public utilities, and building services; the remainder are with the government or with educational institutions.

How Much Money Will I Make?

In 1984, experienced engineers averaged $38,868 a year, and managers made an average of $69,780. The average *starting* salaries for engineers, by branch, were:

Branch	Salary
Petroleum	$29,568
Chemical	$27,420
Electrical	$26,556
Metallurgical	$26,566
Nuclear	$26,388
Mechanical	$26,280
Aeronautical	$25,836
Industrial	$25,221
Mining	$24,876
Civil	$21,764

What Are the Job Opportunities?

Electrical, electronics, and mechanical engineers are in the top 20 fastest growing careers. The opportunities in engineering will continue to be excellent through the 1980s. Engineering students, who make up about 7 percent of the total number of college graduates, received 65 percent of the job offers. Even though only 5 percent of all engineers are women, they make up 15 to 25 percent of engineering students. Purdue University, one of the most active recruiters for women, enrolls 20 percent women, and at Princeton the number of women engineering students is growing. All students interested in engineering must get the required mathematics and physics in high school to qualify for an engineering program in college. Engineering is one of the few professions that does not require a graduate degree. Young women should get in on the advantages of this high-paying career that has plenty of job opportunities. It takes the same number of years of college as teaching, and pays double the money!

Related Careers

Environmental scientist   Mathematician
Physical scientist   Architect

Where Can I Get More Information?

Engineers' Council for Professional Development
345 East 47th Street
New York, New York 10017

Society of Women Engineers
United Engineering Center
345 East 47th Street
New York, New York 10017

ENVIRONMENTALIST

**Studies the earth's water, interior, and
atmosphere, and the environment in space**

What's It Like To Be an Environmentalist?

"Environmentalists," writes a geologist, "share many methods
with other fields of science—the collection of evidence leading to
new conclusions, the application of all available techniques to
test a hypothesis, and the thrill of discovery. In addition, they
have certain satisfactions peculiar to themselves—the immediacy
of using the earth as a laboratory, the healthful exercise of
fieldwork, and the unusual perspective one gets from dealing
familiarly with the immensity of geological time." *Geophysicists*
study the size and shape, interior, surface, and atmosphere of
the earth, the land and bodies of water on its surface and underground, and the atmosphere surrounding it. They often use
satellites to collect and analyze data. *Meteorologists* study the
air that surrounds the earth, including weather patterns. Besides weather forecasting, they work to understand and solve
air pollution problems. *Oceanographers* study the ocean—its
characteristics, movements, plant life, and animal life. Aqua-
culture is an industry for the eighties, where oceanographers
will be in high demand to develop increased fish, food, and
energy resources.

What Education and Skills Will I Need?

High school: Preparation for college with emphasis on science and computer science.

College: Major in any environmental science or related science to prepare for graduate work, which is necessary for any scientist.

Computer skills: Skill level 4—READ, ENTER, PRINT, SELECT. This level is required of all scientists.

Personal skills: Curiosity to do new research, an analytical mind, and physical stamina for outdoor life are necessary skills.

How Many Environmentalists Are There and Where Do They Work?

There are 12,000 geophysicists, 4,000 meteorologists, and 2,800 oceanographers. About 10 percent are women. Most environmentalists work for private industry, oil and gas producers in the Southwest, and agencies of the federal government.

How Much Money Will I Make?

In 1984, beginners with a bachelor's degree made $22,800 and with a master's degree started at $29,300 a year in private industry. The median salary for experienced environmentalists with the federal government was $42,000 a year.

What Are the Job Opportunities?

Private industry will be the best bet for environmentalists because the federal government is cutting jobs. Applicants with advanced degrees and summer work experience will have an edge on the competition for available jobs.

Related Careers

Engineer   Geologist
Conservationist

Where Can I Get More Information?

Office of Sea Grant
National Oceanic and Atmospheric Administration
Rockville, Maryland 20852

American Meteorological Society
45 Beacon Street
Boston, Massachusetts 02108

American Geophysical Union
2000 Florida Avenue, NW
Washington, D.C. 20009

GEOLOGIST

Studies the composition, structure, and history of the earth's crust

What's It Like To Be a Geologist?

Geologists analyze information collected through creating earth tremors, which involves bouncing sound waves off deeply buried rock layers; examine surface rocks and samples of buried rocks recovered by drilling; and study information collected by satellites. They also identify rocks and minerals, conduct geological surveys, construct maps, and use instruments such as a gravimeter and magnetometer to measure the earth's gravity and magnetic field. Besides locating oil and minerals, geologists also advise construction companies and government agencies on the suitability of proposed locations for buildings, dams, or highways.

What Education and Skills Will I Need?

High school: Preparation for college with plenty of science.
College: More than 220 universities award advanced degrees in geology and about 70 in geophysics.

Computer skills: Skill level 4—READ, ENTER, PRINT, SELECT. This level is required for research jobs.

Personal skills: Curiosity and ability to analyze and communicate effectively are important skills. Those involved in fieldwork must have physical stamina.

How Many Geologists Are There and Where Do They Work?

There are 49,000 geologists and geophysicists; 7 percent of them are women and 5 percent are black. Most work for oil and gas companies (44 percent), the federal government employs 16 percent, and oil and gas field services employ 14 percent.

How Much Money Will I Make?

Private industry started geologists with master's degrees at $29,300 a year in 1984. Experienced geologists with the federal government had a median salary of $42,000.

What Are the Job Opportunities?

The job opportunities will be good through the 1980s. Geologists will be needed to discover new mineral resources, to devise ways to explore deeper within the earth's crust, and to develop more efficient methods of mining. They also will be needed to develop more adequate water supplies and waste disposal methods, and to do site evaluation for construction activities.

Related Careers

Petroleum engineer   Marine biologist
Meteorologist   Oceanographer

Where Can I Get More Information?

American Geological Institute
4220 King Street
Alexandria, Virginia 22302

MATHEMATICIAN

Creates new mathematical theories and
solves scientific, managerial, engineering,
and social problems in mathematical terms

What's It Like To Be a Mathematician?

Maureen Garofano, a statistician for General Electric, has been
on the job for three years and loves her work solving financial
forecast problems through mathematics. Garofano emphasizes
the importance of doing the best you can in your college subjects
because you never know how you will be using them. "In high
school, I had no intention of doing anything with math! I took
the usual math courses for college, but not until my junior year
in college did I plan to major in statistics." Large manufacturing
firms such as GE, IBM, and Wang offer graduate courses at
nearby universities in quantitative analysis so that employees
can keep upgrading themselves in their careers.

Many young women think that mathematics is a natural for
men. "Not so," says GE mathematician Delbert O. Martin. He
urges high school students to be persistent. Martin says, "Don't
take the first failure seriously. I had to take elementary calculus
three times before I passed it. I like being a mathematician
because my work is exciting, challenging, and creative."

What Education and Skills
Will I Need?

High school: Preparation for college with emphasis in mathematics and computer science. Be sure that you elect fourth-year
and the Advanced Placement mathematics course in high
school.

College: Major in mathematics, or in a related field with a minor
in mathematics, to prepare for an advanced degree in mathematics, which is necessary for research and university teaching
jobs.

Computer skills: Skill level 6—READ, ENTER, PRINT, SELECT,
GRAPHICS, PROGRAM. The highest skill level is required of
all mathematical careers.

Personal skills: Good reasoning ability, persistence, and ability
to apply basic principles to new types of problems are necessary.

How Many Mathematicians Are There and Where Do They Work?

There are 31,000 mathematicians and statisticians. There are so few women and blacks that the U.S. Department of Labor doesn't even count them! Mathematicians and statisticians work for the federal government (30 percent), private industry in manufacturing (20 percent), state government (13 percent), business services (11 percent), and the insurance industry (7 percent).

How Much Money Will I Make?

College graduates started at $23,400 a year in private industry, and a Ph.D. started at $35,600 in 1984. Colleges and government pay slightly less. The average salary for all mathematicians in the federal government was $35,400 a year.

What Are the Job Opportunities?

Jobs in applied mathematics in engineering and technology will be excellent through the 1980s. There is a shortage of Ph.D. mathematicians, which is providing more job opportunities for theoreticians. Statisticians are expanding into new areas such as law and management problems, creating more jobs for graduates. A critical shortage of mathematics teachers is predicted through the 1980s.

Related Careers

Engineer   Actuary
Systems analyst   Statistician

Where Can I Get More Information?

Mathematical Association of America
1529 18th Street, NW
Washington, D.C. 20036

American Statistical Association
806 15th Street, NW
Washington, D.C. 20005

PHYSICIST

Describes in mathematical terms the
fundamental forces and laws of nature, and
the interaction of matter and energy

What's It Like To Be a Physicist?

Through systematic observation and experimentation, physicists use mathematics to describe the basic forces and laws of nature, such as gravity, electromagnetism, and nuclear interaction. Most physicists work in research and development for private industry and the government. They often specialize in areas such as nuclear energy, electronics, communications, aerospace, or medical instrumentation. The flight of the space shuttle and the safety of the family car are dependent upon research by physicists. Physicists have developed lasers (devices that amplify light and emit it in a highly directional, intense beam), which are utilized in surgery; microwave devices that are used for ovens; and measurement instruments that can detect the kind and number of cells in blood or the amount of lead in foods.

What Education and Skills Will I Need?

High school: Preparation for college, with as much mathematics and computer science as possible.

College: Major in physics or mathematics in college to prepare for graduate school. A career physicist must have a Ph.D.

Computer skills: Skill level 6—READ, ENTER, PRINT, SELECT, GRAPHICS, PROGRAM. The highest level of skills is required for most physicists' work.

Personal skills: Mathematical ability, an inquisitive mind, and imagination plus the ability to think in abstract terms are needed to be a physicist.

How Many Physicists Are There and Where Do They Work?

There are 20,000 physicists and very few are women or black. Most work for the federal government (30 percent); others work for private research labs (21 percent), consulting for engineering and architectural firms (15 percent), and for electronics manufacturing firms (12 percent).

How Much Money Will I Make?

Beginning physicists in private industry with a master's degree started at $30,000 a year, and with a Ph.D. at $37,500 in 1984.

What Are the Job Opportunities?

Jobs in physics are expected to be good through the 1980s, although competitive in astronomy (a related field, usually prepared for by majoring in physics). Graduates with a Ph.D. will find private industry research the best bet because government is cutting its budgets—including those for space research.

Related Careers

Engineer   Chemist
Mathematician   Geologist

Where Can I Get More Information?

American Institute of Physics
335 East 45th Street
New York, New York 10017

SOCIAL SCIENCE

ABOUT THESE CAREERS

First of all, it's important to know that most social science majors in college do not go into a social science career. What do they do? The same as many liberal arts students—they go into business, sales, and management. They go into the arts, law, education, and many, into government.

Second, it's encouraging to know that in 1985 social science graduates got higher salary offers—an indication that employers are looking more favorably on liberal arts degrees—than they did in the early 1980s. The average yearly salary for a college graduate with a social science degree in psychology, anthropology, government, or women's studies was $18,540 a year.

The trend in some industries is to hire increasing numbers of social science majors as trainees for administrative and executive positions. Research councils and other nonprofit organizations provide an important source of employment for economists, political scientists, and sociologists.

Every liberal arts college in the country offers majors in most of the social sciences. The choice of a graduate school is important for people who want to be social scientists. Students interested in research should select schools that emphasize training in research, statistics, and computers.

Social science is a career field where a Ph.D. is needed for many entry-level positions and for almost all of the top jobs. Other than economists, most social scientists work in colleges and universities where the job market for Ph.D.s has crashed.

Working conditions in the social sciences are very good, because most colleges provide excellent benefit plans with sabbatical leaves of absence, life and health insurance, and retirement plans. Working hours for professors are generally flexible. Professors with tenure have security and prestige. The biggest problem is finding employment. In other words, it's nice work—if you can get it. Clinical and counseling psychologists often work in the evenings, since their patients are sometimes unable to leave their jobs or school during the work day.

Social science is one of the most overcrowded career groups. If social science is where you want to be, prepare for applied science by acquiring computer and management skills.

ANTHROPOLOGIST

Studies people—their origins, physical characteristics, customs, languages, traditions, material possessions, structured social relationships, and value systems

What's It Like To Be an Anthropologist?

Anthropologists usually specialize in cultural anthropology (sometimes called ethnology), archaeology, linguistics, or physical anthropology. *Ethnologists* may spend long periods (sometimes years) living in primitive villages to learn a people's way of life. Sometimes their studies include complex urban societies as well. *Archaeologists* dig for past civilizations. They excavate and study the remains of homes, tools, ornaments, and evidence of activity, in order to reconstruct the people's history and customs. *Linguists* scientifically study the sounds and structures of languages and the relationship between language and people's behavior. *Physical anthropologists* study human evolution by comparing the physical characteristics of different races or groups of people. Related to these basic areas of study are subfields of applied, urban, and medical anthropology. Anthropologist Dr. William E. Mitchell, specialist in ethnology, took his family, including two preschool children, to the bush of New Guinea for two years. Mitchell encourages young people to be anthropologists if they "have an insatiable curiosity about people and the patience and tact to study first-hand the different ways—often strange to us—that human groups have arranged to live their lives. What delights me most about being an anthropologist," says Mitchell, "is the fact that the problems are so immense and the factors so complex for understanding human behavior that it will always elude my grasp. I may sometimes be frustrated but *never* bored with my work."

What Education and Skills Will I Need?

High school: Strong college preparatory course to prepare for a competitive liberal arts program.

College: Liberal arts degree to prepare for graduate work. Most anthropologists major in a social science, although you don't have to be an anthropology major in your undergraduate work. A Ph.D. in anthropology is required for a professional career in a university or in research.

Computer skills: Skill level 2—READ, ENTER. All social scientists need to be able to read and enter on a terminal. Most use a word processor and need level 4.

Personal skills: Reading, research, and writing skills are essential, as well as an interest in detail and an ability to work independently.

How Many Anthropologists Are There and Where Do They Work?

There are 7,200 anthropologists and half are women. Almost all work in universities, although some are employed by museums and the government.

How Much Money Will I Make?

In 1984, starting salaries in college teaching for beginners with a Ph.D. averaged $19,200 a year. Full professors averaged $39,000. Many anthropologists supplement their teaching salaries with grants for research in the summer, field trips for students, and summer school teaching.

What Are the Job Opportunities?

There are virtually no jobs for anthropologists. All college teaching jobs are competitive as student enrollments decrease. Very limited opportunities will be available in museums or research programs because federal and university spending is down and the number of Ph.D.s in anthropology has been up for years.

Related Careers

Sociologist   Community planner
Psychologist   Reporter

Where Can I Get More Information?

American Anthropological Association
1703 New Hampshire Avenue, NW
Washington, D.C. 20009

ECONOMIST

**Studies how goods and services are
produced, distributed, and consumed**

What's It Like To Be an Economist?

An economist deals with the relationship between supply and demand for goods and services. Some work in specific fields, such as control of inflation, prevention of economic depression, and development of farm, wage, and tax policies. Others develop theories to explain causes of employment and unemployment, international trade influences, and world economic conditions. Economist Anne Kahl, U.S. Department of Labor, collects data and assesses economic trends through employment in America.

She specializes in the analysis of women and older workers in the work force. Her analysis includes data on prices, wages, employment, and productivity. Ms. Kahl keeps up with current economic theory through her graduate studies at George Washington University.

What Education and Skills Will I Need?

High school: Preparation for college, with as strong a program as is offered in high school.

College: Major in economics or a related social science, or mathematics with computer science or statistics to prepare for an advanced degree in economics. A Ph.D. is required for the top teaching or research jobs.

Computer skills: Skill level 6—READ, ENTER, PRINT, SELECT, GRAPHICS, PROGRAM. Economists require proficiency for the complexity of mathematical variables involved in their research.

Personal skills: Ability and interest in detailed, accurate research is needed. Most economists must be able to express themselves well in writing.

How Many Economists Are There and Where Do They Work?

Of the 30,000 economists, 28 percent are women and 5 percent are black. Almost half of them work for the government (45 percent), 20 percent teach in college, and 10 percent work in business. Most are employed in New York and Washington.

How Much Money Will I Make?

New graduates with a Ph.D. averaged $20,000 a year in 1984. Economists with experience averaged $24,300 to $41,700 in business. The top 10 percent make more than $52,000. Economics professors make the same as other college professors.

What Are the Job Opportunities?

Jobs will be very competitive through the 1980s. The best chances will be for those who are skilled in computer and quantitative techniques and their application to economic modeling and forecasting.

Related Careers

Actuary   Bank officer
Accountant   Stockbroker

Where Can I Get More Information?

American Economic Association
1313 21st Avenue South
Nashville, Tennessee 37212

American Marketing Association
250 South Wacker Drive
Chicago, Illinois 60606

GEOGRAPHER

**Studies the physical characteristics of the
earth—its terrain, minerals, soils, water,
vegetation, and climate**

What's It Like To Be a Geographer?

Geographers analyze maps and aerial photographs, and also
construct maps, graphs, and diagrams. They analyze the distribution and structure of political organizations, transportation systems, and marketing systems. Mike Taupier, a 30-year-
old graduate student in geography, is looking for a job in the
ecological sciences. "Geography," says Taupier, "isn't as popular
as many other sciences and the job market is better. It fits into
work with both physical and social sciences, and is often related
to work in botany, geology, political science, and history." Many
geographers have job titles, such as cartographer, map analyst,
or regional planner, that describe their specialization. Others
have titles that relate to their subject matter, such as photoin-
telligence specialist or climatological analyst. Still others have
titles such as community planner and market or business
analyst.

What Education and Skills Will I Need?

High school: Preparation for college, with emphasis on all social and biological sciences.

College: Graduate work is required for a career in geography. There are 56 universities offering a Ph.D. in geography.

Computer skills: Skill level 4—READ, ENTER, PRINT, SELECT. All scientists need word processing skills, and more proficiency is desirable as a research tool.

Personal skills: Reading, studying, computing, and research skills are needed, along with an interest in working independently.

How Many Geographers Are There and Where Do They Work?

There are 15,000 geographers and 15 percent are women. Most of them teach in colleges; the remainder are with the government, primarily in the Department of Defense and Department of the Interior.

How Much Money Will I Make?

In 1984, a graduate with a master's degree started with the federal government at $21,800 a year; a Ph.D. graduate started at $26,400. Cartographers with the federal government averaged slightly more.

What Are the Job Opportunities?

The outlook through the 1980s for work is better than for most social scientists. Those with computer skills and training in cartography, satellite data interpretation, or planning will have the best chances for a job.

Related Careers

Engineer   Oceanographer
Geologist   Meteorologist

Where Can I Get More Information?

Association of American Geographers
1710 16th Street, NW
Washington, D.C. 20009

HISTORIAN

**Studies the records of the past and analyzes
events, institutions, ideas, and people**

What's It Like To Be a Historian?

Historians relate their knowledge of the past to current events
in an effort to explain the present. They may specialize in the
history of a specific country or area, or a particular period of
time, such as ancient, medieval, or modern. They also may specialize in the history of a field, such as economics, culture, the
labor movement, art, or architecture. The number of specialities
in history is constantly growing. Newer specialties are concerned with business archives, quantitative analysis, and the
relationship between technological and other aspects of historical development. A growing number of historians now specialize in African, Latin American, Chinese, Asian, or Near Eastern
history. For example, Harvey J. Spalding, Ph.D., a black man,
majored in African history in college. He now works for a black
historical society that is seeking new understandings about mi-
norities in America. Other specialties include archivists, who
are associated with museums, special libraries, and historical
societies. Women's history is the fastest growing specialty in
the profession. Just 15 years ago, the field of women's history
did not exist. Today, there are over 1,000 women and men who
work exclusively in the field. The annual conference on the
history of women has as many attendees as the American Historical Association.

What Education and Skills
Will I Need?

High school: Preparation for college, with a strong social science background.

College: Most historians major in history, with minors in government, economics, sociology, or anthropology. A doctorate is necessary for a career in college teaching and for better government jobs.

Computer skills: Skill level 4—READ, ENTER, PRINT, SELECT. Social scientists need to be able to use a word processor for research and reports.

Personal skills: An interest in reading, studying, and research and the ability to write papers and reports are necessary for historians.

How Many Historians Are There and Where Do They Work?

There are about 20,000 historians and 20 percent are women. Seventy percent of all historians work in colleges and universities, with others employed by the government, archives, libraries, museums, and historical societies.

How Much Money Will I Make?

College instructors averaged $19,200 a year in 1984, and full professors $39,900. Museum curators with a Ph.D. averaged $26,400 a year for an entry-level position.

What Are the Job Opportunities?

Historians will find stiff competition in all employment opportunities through the 1980s. There are many more Ph.D.s in history than there are jobs for them. People with computer skills are expected to have the best chance for a job in business and research.

Related Careers

Political scientist   Sociologist
Economist   Journalist

Where Can I Get More Information?

American Historical Association
400 A Street, SE
Washington, D.C. 20003

POLITICAL SCIENTIST

Studies how political power is gained and used

What's It Like To Be a Political Scientist?

Most political scientists teach in colleges and universities, where they combine research, consultation, or administration with teaching. Many specialize in a general area of political science such as political theory, U.S. political institutions and processes, comparative political processes, or international relations. Joseph and Maria Manelli are graduate students in political science. They plan to work together doing research for a private firm that surveys public opinion on political questions. They can also use their research skills to study proposed legislation for reference bureaus and congressional committees. Manelli and Manelli hope to start their own legislative research service eventually.

What Education and Skills Will I Need?

High school: Preparation for college, with an emphasis on history, government, and the social sciences.

College: Major in political science or in a related major, such as government, history, or economics, to prepare for graduate work. Almost all political scientists have a master's degree for a beginning job, and a Ph.D. is required for a career in political science. Law school is an alternative to a Ph.D.

Computer skills: Skill level 4—READ, ENTER, PRINT, SELECT. All social scientists require minimum word processing skills, and often need graphics for statistical research and reports.

Personal skills: Political scientists must have an interest in details, be as objective as possible in their thinking, and have good oral and writing skills.

How Many Political Scientists Are There and Where Do They Work?

There are about 15,000 political scientists; very few are women or blacks. Three-fourths of them teach in college. Others are employed by government agencies, political organizations, public interest groups, labor unions, and research institutes.

How Much Money Will I Make?

In 1984 a political scientist with a Ph.D. averaged $19,200 a year as a college instructor. Government political scientists with a master's degree started at $21,800.

What Are the Job Opportunities?

Employment opportunities are very competitive in college teaching, business, and government. A political science degree is helpful for a career in journalism, foreign affairs, law, or other related work. Well-qualified political scientists with computer skills will have the best chances in applied fields.

Related Careers

Politician	Lawyer
Historian	Sociologist

Where Can I Get More Information?

American Political Science Association
1527 New Hampshire Avenue, NW
Washington, D.C. 20036

PSYCHOLOGIST

Studies the behavior of individuals and groups in order to understand and explain their actions

What's It Like To Be a Psychologist?

A clinical psychologist working in a mental health clinic spends most of the time testing clients with individual psychological tests and scoring the tests. He or she meets with the clinical team of social worker, psychiatrist, and educator to interpret the test scores and determine ways to help the individual. A psychologist often works with group therapy classes of young parents, adolescents, children, or whatever group needs therapy in the particular community or agency. She or he has conferences with parents, community leaders, and educators about clients in common, and tries to get all groups to make a joint effort toward helping a person in stress.

What Education and Skills Will I Need?

High school: Preparation for college, with a science, computer science, and social science emphasis.

College: Major in psychology, although many students major in a related field such as sociology, anthropology, or education, and prepare for graduate work in psychology. A master's degree is required for most practical work in psychology, including school psychologist, psychologist in a government agency, and mental health work. A Ph.D. is required for research, college training jobs, and promotions in many jobs.

Computer skills: Skill level 3—READ, ENTER, PRINT. If research is your goal, you will need skill level 4, SELECT, as well.

Personal skills: Sensitivity to others and a genuine interest in people are important for counseling. Research jobs require an interest in detail, accuracy, and writing skills.

How Many Psychologists Are There and Where Do They Work?

There are 97,000 psychologists; 55 percent are women and 8 percent are black. Most (41 percent) work for schools, 15 percent work for hospitals, and 12 percent for state and federal government agencies.

How Much Money Will I Make?

In 1984 the average annual salary for a psychologist working for the federal government with a doctoral degree was $39,800, and $21,800 with a master's. Self-employed psychologists who do consulting work and see patients privately earned much more, often up to $100,000 a year in major cities. Ph.D.s in business and industry averaged $48,000 a year.

What Are the Job Opportunities?

There will be many more Ph.D.s in psychology than job openings through the 1980s. Tight school and government budgets and an overload of Ph.D.s make jobs almost impossible with only a bachelor's or master's degree.

Related Careers

Psychiatrist   Social worker
School counselor   Clergy

Where Can I Get More Information?

American Psychological Association
1200 17th Street, NW
Washington, D.C. 20036

SOCIOLOGIST

Studies the behavior and interaction of people in groups

What's It Like To Be a Sociologist?

Sociologist Dr. Hope Jensen Leichter, professor at Columbia University, says, "My interest in sociology is to provide the significant theory about how people are affected by their families, by their schools, and by their work, so that professionals in the helping careers, such as social workers, educators, and nurses, will have some idea of what makes people behave as they do." America has every kind of group of people, and the possibilities for research are limited only by a lack of imagination. Some sociologists study the causes of social problems such as crime or poverty, the pattern of family relations, or the different patterns of living in communities of varying types and sizes. Increasingly, sociologists are working in prison systems, education, industrial public relations, and regional and community planning.

What Education and Skills Will I Need?

High school: Preparation for college, with a strong academic program and computer skills.

College: Major in any social science and prepare for graduate work in sociology. A Ph.D. is required for a career in sociology.

Computer skills: Skill level 4—READ, ENTER, PRINT, SELECT. Researchers in the social sciences require word processing and often use graphics as well.

Personal skills: Study and research skills are crucial for the sociologist, as are communication skills, especially writing.

How Many Sociologists Are There and Where Do They Work?

There are 5,600 sociologists, and about half are women. Many (20 percent) work for state governments, and another 20 percent work in hospitals, 12 percent are professors, and 14 percent work for local government.

How Much Money Will I Make?

The median annual salary for a social scientist with a doctorate was $31,800 in 1984. Industry paid $36,300 a year, the federal government $38,700. College professors started at $19,200 and averaged $39,900 as full professors.

What Are the Job Opportunities?

College jobs are very competitive and there will be thousands of Ph.D.s in sociology and no job openings through the 1980s. Most sociologists go on to graduate school or go into another career area. (*See* Odd Jobs.)

Related Careers

Anthropologist   Political scientist
Historian   Community planner

Where Can I Get More Information?

American Sociological Association
1772 N Street, NW
Washington, D.C. 20036

SOCIAL SERVICE

ABOUT THESE CAREERS

Social service jobs require more education for less pay than any other field of work except education. There are over 732,000 social service jobs. Concern for people, not desire for money, is needed to be happy in the social services. Patience, tact, sensitivity, and compassion are necessary personal qualities.

In social service careers, there are a great variety of settings and tasks. Depending on their specific occupation, workers may advise consumers on how to get the most for their money; help people with disabilities to achieve satisfactory lifestyles; provide religious services; counsel people having problems in their job, home, school, or social relationships; or treat people with emotional problems.

Although there are different types of social service jobs, many of them require some of the same skills. In general, a knowledge of the field is gained through a college degree. One to three years of graduate work in a professional school are required for many social service careers such as counseling, clergy, and social work.

Beginning counselors and social workers who have little experience are assigned the less difficult cases. As they gain experience, their caseloads are increased and they are assigned clients with more complex problems. After getting experience and more graduate education, rehabilitation counselors and social workers may advance to supervisory positions or top administrative jobs.

After a few years of experience, recreation leaders may become supervisors. Although promotions to administrative jobs may be easier with graduate training, advancement is still possible through a combination of education and experience.

Social service jobs usually involve irregular hours because the workers provide a wide range of services to people in many circumstances. For example, the clergy must go to people whenever they are in crisis, as well as visit regularly. Recreation workers can expect night work and irregular hours, since they often have to work while others are enjoying leisure time.

Social service jobs often depend on government spending, because so many of the programs are tied to federal budgets. When money is tight and budgets are cut, as is true in the 1980s, the job situation becomes a very tough one.

CLERGY

Jewish, Roman Catholic, and Protestant religious clergy serve the spiritual needs of their people and provide a moral and ethical model in the wider community in which they live

What's It Like To Be a Member of the Clergy?

Young people who choose to enter the ministry, priesthood, or rabbinate do so mainly because they have a strong religious faith and a desire to help others. Deciding on a career in the clergy involves considerations different from other career choices. In addition to the clergy who serve in congregations and parishes, there are teachers and administrators in education; chaplains in the military, prisons, hospitals, and on college campuses; and missionaries and those who serve in social welfare agencies.

Protestant ministers lead their congregations in worship services and administer the rites of baptism, confirmation, and Holy Communion. They prepare and deliver sermons, and give religious instruction to new members of the church.

Rabbis are the spiritual leaders of their congregations, and teachers and interpreters of Jewish law and tradition. They conduct religious services and deliver sermons on the Sabbath and on Jewish holidays. Rabbis serve either Orthodox, Conservative, or Reform congregations. They differ in the extent to which they follow the traditional form of worship, for example, in wearing head coverings, in using Hebrew as the language of prayer, or in using music and a choir.

Roman Catholic priests attend to the spiritual, pastoral, moral, and educational needs of the members of their church. Their duties include presiding at liturgical functions, delivering sermons, hearing confessions, and administering the sacraments. There are two main classifications of priests—diocesan (secular) and religious. Diocesan priests generally work as individuals in parishes assigned to them by the bishop of their diocese. Religious priests generally work as part of a religious order, such as Jesuits, Dominicans, or Franciscans. They engage in specialized work assigned to them by superiors in their order, such as teaching or social work.

All clergy conduct weddings and funeral services, visit the sick, help the poor, comfort the bereaved, supervise religious educational programs, engage in interfaith activities, and involve themselves in community affairs. Clergy serving smaller churches or synagogues usually work on a personal basis with their parishioners. Those serving large congregations have greater administrative responsibilities. They spend a lot of time working with committees, church officers, and staff, in addition to performing many community duties. They often have one or more associates who share specific aspects of the ministry, and who help them meet the individual needs of parishioners.

What Education and Skills Will I Need?

High school: Preparation for a strong liberal arts college program.

College: Major in religion or theology, or any related field that deals with understanding people, as preparation for a master's degree in divinity for Protestants, a three- to five-year seminary program for Jews, and a four-year seminary program for Catholics.

Computer skills: Skill level 4—READ, ENTER, PRINT, SELECT. Being able to use the word processor is important for writing and preparing budgets and programs.

Personal skills: Religious careers require a deep commitment to the religious and spiritual needs of people, and the ability to fulfill that commitment through the spiritual leadership of others.

How Many Clergy Are There and Where Do They Work?

There are 416,000 Protestant ministers, 252,000 of whom are in churches serving 72 million people. About 1,110 Orthodox, 800 Conservative, and 6,500 Reform rabbis serve 6 million Jews. There are 58,000 priests and an additional 6,700 lay deacons serving 49 million Catholics. Only 5 percent of all clergy are women and 6 percent are black. Every community in America has at least one Protestant church with a full-time minister. Most work for the five largest churches—Baptist, Methodist, Lutheran, Presbyterian, and Pentecostal. Rabbis are concentrated in the major cities of America that have large Jewish populations. There are priests in nearly every city and town in America, although the majority are in metropolitan areas.

How Much Money Will I Make?

In 1984 the average salary for Protestant ministers was about $18,000 a year plus housing; $25,000 to $75,000 for rabbis; and a stipend of $4,000 to $8,000 plus all maintenance expenses for priests, who take a vow of poverty.

What Are the Job Opportunities?

Jobs for Protestant and Jewish clergy will continue to be competitive through the 1980s as congregations decrease and the number of seminarians goes up. Conservative and Reform rabbis will have the best chance for jobs. Catholic priests are in demand because of a sharp drop in seminary enrollment. Jobs for women continue to be very difficult because of discrimination against women in the clergy. Since 1973, 111 Jewish Reformed women have been ordained and the first Conservative Jewish woman, Rabbi Amy Eilberg, was ordained in 1985. It was only ten years ago that Episcopalians ordained women. Catholics have yet to admit women to their clergy.

Related Careers

Social worker	Chaplain
Counselor	Missionary

Where Can I Get More Information?

Your local church or synagogue can give you the name and address of the headquarters of your religious group for career information.

> National Catholic Vocation Council
> 1307 South Wabash Avenue
> Chicago, Illinois 60605 (Catholic)

> Hebrew Union College—Jewish Institute of Religion
> 3101 Clifton Avenue
> Cincinnati, Ohio 45220 (Reform Jewish)

> The Rabbi Isaac Elchanan Theological Seminary
> 2540 Amsterdam Avenue
> New York, New York 10033 (Orthodox Jewish)

> Jewish Theological Seminary of America
> 3080 Broadway
> New York, New York 10027 (Conservative Jewish)

> National Council of Churches
> Professional Church Leadership
> 475 Riverside Drive, Room 770
> New York, New York 10027

RECREATION WORKER

**Helps people develop good physical and
mental health through recreation and
group activity within an organization**

What's It Like To Be a Recreation Worker?

Recreation workers organize activities for all ages and interests at local recreation programs, community centers, churches, hospitals, camps, and playgrounds. The major youth agencies are the Boy Scouts and Girl Scouts, YWCA and YMCA, 4-H

Clubs, Red Cross, and American Youth Hostels. These organizations help people to use and enjoy their leisure time constructively through physical, social, and cultural programs. Recreation directors lead classes and discussions, teach skills, take charge of hikes and trips, and direct programs and camps. They operate recreational facilities and study recreational needs of individuals and communities. Garcia and Pam Rodriguez are the camp directors of a coed camp for sailing. They met as camp counselors, married, and went into the recreation business. They have developed a year-round business promoting, recruiting, and operating their camp for teenagers. They each worked for several agencies before they decided to go into business for themselves. Both physical education majors, Garcia is working on his master's in recreation, and Pam is getting her advanced degree in business administration.

What Education and Skills Will I Need?

High school: Preparation for community college or four-year college.

College: Half of the professional recreation workers are college graduates. Community college graduates also have good employment opportunities in recreation work. A major in physical education, recreation, or social sciences, and a master's degree are necessary for many administration jobs.

Computer skills: Skill level 2—READ, ENTER. This basic level is required to read the terminal and enter data. Many recreation people who use the computer for scheduling and game strategies need more skills.

Personal skills: Skill in sports, music, and crafts; creativity and enthusiasm about activities; and good judgment are necessary for success in recreation.

How Many Recreation Workers Are There and Where Do They Work?

There are 124,000 recreation workers; 62 percent are women, and 13 percent are black. About 27 percent are employed part time. Many work for local government (38 percent), others for major recreational organizations (22 percent), and still others for social services (13 percent) and nursing homes (10 percent).

How Much Money Will I Make?

In 1984, beginners with a college degree made from $15,000 to $19,000 a year. Community supervisors of recreation were in the range of $20,500 to $26,000.

What Are the Job Opportunities?

Recreation jobs for local government will continue to be competitive because of tight budgets. Jobs are increasing in nursing homes and in community centers for older people. There is a great demand for part-time recreation and coaching jobs in the public schools.

Related Careers

Club manager   Camp director
Physical education teacher   Physical therapist

Where Can I Get More Information?

National Recreation and Park Association
3101 Park Central Drive
Arlington, Virginia 22302

American Camping Association
Bradford Woods
Martinsville, Indiana 46151

REHABILITATION COUNSELOR

Assists physically, mentally, and
emotionally disabled persons in making a
satisfactory occupational adjustment

What's It Like To Be a Rehabilitation Counselor?

Rehabilitation counselors evaluate their clients' potential for jobs and arrange medical care, rehabilitation programs, occupational training, and job placement. Norma McNall of Ardmore, Oklahoma, says, "I work out a plan of rehabilitation after consulting with the person's social worker, medical doctor, and sometimes the family. Most of my work is done with alcoholics, although some of my coworkers specialize with the mentally ill or retarded, and others help any person who can't adjust to a job. I keep in contact with my clients' employers and look for more employers who will hire the disabled. The amount of direct counseling varies with each person, but we try to involve family and other agencies in helping the person as she or he tries to get back to work on a regular basis."

What Education and Skills Will I Need?

High school: Preparation for college, with emphasis on the social sciences.

College: Major in education, psychology, guidance, or sociology to prepare for graduate school. A master's degree in psychology, student personnel, vocational counseling, or rehabilitation counseling is usually required.

Computer skills: Skill level 2—READ, ENTER. All service personnel have to be able to read the terminal and enter new data.

Personal skills: Ability to accept responsibility, work independently, and motivate those who may progress very slowly are all necessary to be successful in rehabilitation.

How Many Counselors Are There and Where Do They Work?

There are about 30,000 rehabilitation counselors; about half of them are women and 10 percent are black. Most of them work for state or local rehabilitation agencies. The rest work in hospitals, for labor unions, insurance companies, and sheltered workshops.

How Much Money Will I Make?

Schools paid an average of $27,593 a year for counselors, and other agencies paid slightly less.

What Are the Job Opportunities?

Counselors with a master's degree are expected to have fair job opportunities through the 1980s. Services are needed but federal spending for these jobs is low and getting worse. The best opportunities are in private industry, working with the increasing number of alcohol and drug abusers.

Related Careers

School counselor
Social worker

Occupational therapist
Clergy

Where Can I Get More Information?

National Rehabilitation Counseling Association
633 South Washington Street
Alexandria, Virginia 22314

SOCIAL WORKER

Helps people, families, and groups solve their problems

What's It Like To Be a Social Worker?

Social workers plan and conduct activities for children, adolescents, families, and older people in a variety of settings including settlement houses, hospitals, and correctional institutions. They try to strengthen family life and improve its functioning. They work to improve the physical and emotional well-being of deprived and troubled children. They advise parents on child care and work with school social workers and community leaders. School social workers are employed in the public schools; medical social workers work in hospitals; and psychiatric social workers work in mental health centers and clinics. Cy Abdelnour, 30-year-old social worker for a state agency, prefers working with children. He feels that chances are better for changes in attitude and behavior in a child's life than in an adult's. Abdelnour works with children in school, courts, and child centers. He often visits children at their homes after school, and his evenings include taking clients to sports events and school plays.

What Education and Skills Will I Need?

High school: Preparation for college, with as broad an education as possible.

College: Major in one of the social sciences to prepare for graduate school, or take a bachelor's degree in social work (BSW). A master's degree (MSW), offered in 89 colleges, is required to be a professional member of the National Association of Social Workers.

Computer skills: Skill level 2—READ, ENTER. Ability to read and enter new data is necessary. Many social workers need more skills to use the word processor for reports.

Personal skills: To be happy in social work you must be sensitive to others, as objective as possible, and have a basic concern for people and their problems.

How Many Social Workers Are There and Where Do They Work?

There are 345,000 social workers; 65 percent are women, 17 percent are black. They work mostly for local (25 percent) or state (24 percent) government, or for private social service agencies (22 percent).

How Much Money Will I Make?

The average starting salary for a social worker with a bachelor's degree was $15,700 a year in 1984. A social worker with a master's degree and one year's experience earned $19,300 a year. The federal government paid people with a master's degree an average of $25,500.

What Are the Job Opportunities?

Chances for a job are expected to improve to the 1990s with social work graduates decreasing and need for services increasing with the older population, higher unemployment, and fewer government programs. As governments cut budgets, most job opportunities will be with private agencies, nursing homes, hospices, rehabilitation programs, health maintenance organizations, and home health programs.

Related Careers

Clergy   Counselor
Rehabilitation counselor

Where Can I Get More Information?

National Association of Social Workers
7981 Eastern Avenue
Silver Spring, Maryland 20910